CONTENTS

PREFACE

The aim of this small book is to help all those who wish to become better acquainted with grasses and grass-like plants.

Grasses do not have large or colourful flowers to attract one's attention, but for those who care to look closer at these plants, a wealth of delicate shapes and beauty is revealed.

Until now grasses have been somewhat neglected in our popular, illustrated, botanical works. The reason is that it is far easier to learn and recognise the conspicuous wild flowers than to become acquainted with those plants which form the green background to the vegetation. One's powers of observation and attention to detail need to be developed before one can fully appreciate grasses.

This book covers not only the wild, but also the cultivated species of grasses, i.e. to include cereals and the fodder grasses which have great economic importance. Furthermore, the rushes and sedges have also been included since in everyday usage one groups them with the 'grasses' and not with the 'herbs'.

The range of grasses, sedges and rushes has been made as wide as possible with no less than 147 different species illustrated in the coloured plates. Many of the grass-like plants likely to be found growing in the British Isles have been described and illustrated. Only the less common species have been omitted.

As it is the small details which have such importance in the identification of these plants, great attention has been paid to their descriptions and the text has been supplemented with detailed drawings of features that cannot be shown on the plates.

All plants on the same colour plate are illustrated to the same scale which is usually $\frac{2}{3}$ of the natural size. However, the larger plants are reproduced to half their natural size, but here again, the scale is consistent within the plate.

INTRODUCTION

Grass-like Plants

The expression 'grass-like plants' hardly needs an explanation. In popular botanical classification, there are two different terms, 'grasses' and 'herbs', and these together can cover almost all herbaceous plants which grow in the field.

That 'corn' belongs to the grasses is self-explanatory and it is just as logical that legumes and kitchen herbs belong with the 'herbs'. Naturally a few borderline cases exist which are difficult to classify in this popular division. Chives, for example, have grass-like leaves, but on account of their smell, taste and floral structure, it seems only logical to include it in the 'herbs'.

The common features which characterise the grass-like plants are their straight culms or stems, the long narrow leaves and the insignificant flowers grouped together at the top of the stem. These common characteristics make it easy on the one hand to see what are called 'grasses' in the word's broadest and popular sense, and conversely what can be termed 'herbs'. On the other hand, it is the possession of these common characteristics which make it difficult to distinguish the different species of grasses. Admittedly at times it can be extremely difficult to identify a particular type of grass and the aim of this book is to make identification and classification a little easier.

Looking at the colour plates one should be able to identify many of the grass-like plants likely to be found in the British Isles. When one has found an illustration which looks like the plant at hand, one should read the appropriate description to check its identity.

It should be remembered that many of the described morphological features can hardly be seen by the naked eye, so it is useful to have a magnifying glass to see the finer details of the plant. A pin, or pointed tweezers are particularly useful for separating the various parts.

Grass-like plants can be divided into three plant families; the true Grasses (family Gramineae), the Sedges (family Cyperaceae) and the Rushes (family Juncaceae). In the following section details are given on the relationships of these three plant families with other flowering plant groups, then each of them is discussed individually.

In the individual sections, the technical botanical terms used in the decriptions later in the book are explained. Therefore, it would be advisable to read these sections before referring to the descriptions of particular species. To profit most from the study of these sections, it would be wise to have a plant sample from each of the families to compare with the text and drawings.

The Classification of Grasses, Sedges and Rushes

Flowering plants can be divided into major classes, known as the Monocotyledons and the Dicotyledons. All of the grass-like plants belong to the former group, the Monocotyledons. Monocotyledonous plants are all trimerous plants which means that they can be identified easily, amongst other things, by the flower parts which are predominantly in threes, whilst in Dicotyledons they are predominantly in fives.

As the class names would suggest, Monocotyledons emerge from the seed with only one seed-leaf, and the Dicotyledons with two. In addition, the radicle of Monocotyledons is soon replaced by adventitious roots, which together form fibrous roots and as a general rule their leaves are parallel- or curve-veined and have a simple shape. They are long and narrow (grass-like) or oval with numerous, straight, strongly developed veins or ribs. In the Dicotyledons, by contrast, the radicle often develops into a tap-root and the leaves are often feather- or palmately-veined and have divided margins. Another characteristic of Monocotyledons which should be mentioned is that nearly all of them are herbs. Certain exotic Monocotyledon species can be trees, e.g. palms and the dragon trees which can be many years old and grow a thick trunk, but their habit of growth differs from Dicotyledonous trees. In other words, they do not have a continuing meristem which each year forms a new annual ring of woody tissue, but random meristems which form only soft, secondary tissues.

Within the Monocotyledons, the grass-like plants all belong to the same subclass, namely the Commelinidae, one of four subclasses. Plants which belong to his group have, for the most part, narrow- and parallel-veined leaves, the bases of which are developed into reed-shaped sheaths which encase the hollow stem (culm). More primitive members of the group are plants with well-developed, coloured flowers which are pollinated by insects. But in the more advanced species there is a reduction in flower structure and these are self-pollinated or pollinated by the wind.

Within the subclass Commelinidae the three 'grass-like' plant families are sufficiently different to be considered to belong to two different orders. The true grasses (Gramineae) and the Sedges (Cyperaceae) belong to the order Cyperales and the Rushes, (Juncaceae) belong to the order Juncales.

The two orders represent distinct stages of evolution with regard to the reduction of flowers. Rushes remain closer to the primitive types of the Commelinidae since they have fully developed flowers. Grasses, by contrast, are the most derived since they have very reduced flowers.

As the grasses are the most important and best known family we will begin with the descriptions and diagrams of them and finish with the rushes.

The grasses, sedges and rushes together comprise about 12,000 of the 17,200 species of the sublcass Commelinidae. In all there are about 250,000 species of flowering plants, so the grass-like plants contribute only about 2·5%. However, by contrast, grass-like plants, particularly the grasses themselves, contribute a much larger proportion of the world's vegetation. Just think of the vast areas of natural meadowland, steppes and tundra which are dominated by grass-like plants, not to mention the cultivated areas of fodder grass and cornfields.

The Grass Family

Grasses are easily distinguished from all other plant groups on account of their characteristic structure and by their greatly simpli-

GRASSES, SEDGES
and
RUSHES
in colour

M. SKYTTE CHRISTIANSEN

Translated by
G. Hartz

Edited and adapted for the English language
by
C. J. Humphries *and* J. R. Press

Illustrations by
Verner Hancke

BLANDFORD PRESS
POOLE   DORSET

First published in Great Britain 1979
Copyright © 1979 Blandford Press Ltd.,
Link House, West Street, Poole, Dorset BH15 1LL

ISBN 0 7137 0945 6

British Library Cataloguing in Publication Data

Humphries, C J
    Grasses, sedges and rushes in colour. – (Blandford
    colour series).
    1. Grasses – Europe – Identification   2. Cyperaceae
    – Identification   3. Juncaceae – Identification
    4. Botany – Europe
    I. Title   II. Press, J R   III. Hancke, Verner
    IV. Christiansen, Mogens Skytte.   Graesser i farver.
    Adaptations
    584′.9′094   QK495.G74

Originally published in Denmark as *Græsser i farver*
World Copyright © 1977 Politikens Forlag A/S Copenhagen

Set in 10/11 pt Baskerville
Printed in Great Britain by
Fletcher and Son Ltd, Norwich
and bound by
Richard Clay (The Chaucer Press) Ltd,
Bungay, Suffolk

fied flowers arranged in spikelets and paniculate inflorescences.

The flowers are adapted to pollination by the wind and, during evolution, grasses have greatly diverged from their sister group which retains the more primitive insect pollinated coloured flowers. As a result, grasses have practically speaking no perianth, but instead are surrounded by modified leaves, the glumes, lemma and palea which protect the flowers during their development and the corn or seed during the ripening period.

The grass family (Gramineae) is one with the most numerous species and is of the greatest importance to man, partly because it supplies 'our daily bread' and because it produces fodder for our livestock and many wild grass-eating animals. Furthermore, many species of grass are used commercially for other purposes, such as the thatching of houses, the production of textiles and paper, and for the extraction of starches, sugar, various edible and aromatic oils and, last but not least, as a raw material in the brewing industry. The grass family comprises about 620 genera with about 10,000 species and is represented in all of the major biomes of the terrestrial world. Even in Antarctica there is a species of grass, although no other flowering plant is known to exist there. In the British Isles, between 150 and 160 species of grass can be found growing wild, representing about 53 different genera. In addition to this, there are numerous cultivated grasses and a number of casual species from abroad, which do not often find suitable habitats to become naturalised in our flora.

Grass Growth and Structure

The majority of grasses are herb-like plants whose height can vary from just a couple of centimetres to 6 metres or more. The tallest indigenous grass is the Common Reed (see 29), whose culm can be up to 3 metres tall. In hot climates tree-like grasses can be found, particularly species of Bamboo (*Bambusa*) whose woody culms can reach a height of 36 metres. Some species of Bamboo can grow extremely quickly because their stems have so many growth points. In fact, one species has been known to increase 41 cm in 24 hours, so one can almost say that it is possible to see the grass grow!

Grass shoots are easily recognised. Their stems or culms are usually hollow along the internodes and solid at the nodes, though some foreign species have pith-filled stems; for example, the crop plants, maize, sugar-cane and Indian millet. All of our indigenous grasses have hollow culms and are most often terete (i.e. with circular cross-section) or more rarely flattened (as for example the Flattened Meadow-Grass, 48). One of the main features, of the

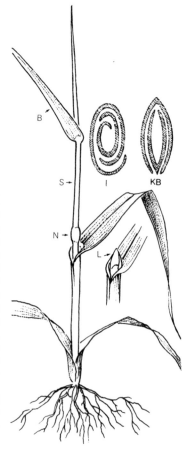

A typical grass stem during growth. A bunch of fibrous roots extends from the base of the culm. The lower culm is invested with older sheaths, whose edges have separated from one another. The sheaths of the younger leaves (S) invest the culms completely in that their edges overlap each other. The sheath is swollen at the base to form the node (N). The leaves are placed in two rows opposite each other up the culm and they have long, linear blades (B). Usually, at the junction between the blade and sheath, a ligule is to be found (L). This is more easily seen when the culm is removed.

The leaf at the top of the shoot has not unfolded yet. It can have inrolled (I), or valvate (V) vernation as shown in the inset detailed drawing.

grass stem is that the culm is divided into obvious sections by the bulbous nodes, occurring at intervals along the stem. The leaves are placed alternately up the culm, emerging at the nodes where the lowest, developing part of the leaf base is to be found.

The blades invest the culm with their sheath. The two edges of the sheath overlap to form a closed tube and in some species the edges of the sheath grow together practically the whole of the way up the stem. This is a particular characteristic of the genera *Bromus*, *Glyceria* and *Melica*.

The upper part of the leaf, the blade, is long and narrow and has parallel (plicate) veins. Grasses which grow in meadows or damp shady places usually have gutter-shaped, or flat, ribbon blades, although in the young condition, they tend to have inrolled blades folded about one margin or around the central nerve. In grasses from dry situations the blades are frequently inrolled or bristle-like and nearly solid except for a groove above. Leaf structure is best seen in the cross-section of a young shoot and it is a good means of identification of a grass when in its vegetative state. All Meadow-Grass species have folded blades, so do Velvet Bent (13) and Perennial Rye Grass (77), whereas Italian Rye Grass (78), Meadow Fescue (55), Meadow Fox-Tail (9), Timothy Grass (6), and Tall Oat-Grass (26) all have inrolled blades.

Blades which have been folded during development will often have two yellowish-green stripes on either side of the mid-rib which one can see by holding them up to the light. These stripes originate from long rows of large, limpid cells, which form an important role

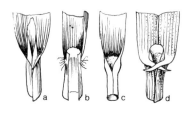

In grasses, the base of the blade and ligule can vary enormously. In some species, the blade narrows evenly at the base (a–c). In others the blade widens at the base and grows two pointed processes (auricles), which invest the culm like a lock (d).

The ligule can be long and pointed (a), or short and truncate (b). Its edge can be even, toothed or fringed. In some species of grass, the ligule has been substituted by a fringe of hairs (c).

in the unfolding of the leaf as they become filled with sap. On blades which have inrolled sheaths one can sometimes see several rows of similar limpid cells which have had their use in the process of unfurling. These are seldom more clearly apparent than in Tufted Hair-Grass (23), where the cells are situated on the thinnest part of the blade between the thick longitudinal ribs. In many grasses a colourless appendage, the ligule, is to be found at the point between the blade and the sheath. However, at times it is replaced by a crown of hairs as in the Common Reed-Grass (29), Purple Moor-Grass (30) and Heath Grass (31) or is absent altogether, as in Cockspur (89). One can best see the ligule by pulling the blade completely away from the culm.

Sometimes pointed outgrowths (auricles) can be found at the base of each side of the blade which invest the culm from each side (see for example, Meadow Fescue, 55, and Couch Grass, 76).

Everyone who has pulled up a piece of grass and chewed the base will know that it is soft and juicy. It is just here, at the base of the culm, that the growing point of the leaf is situated. It is obvious, therefore, why the soft part of the culm is invested by the protective leaf-sheath.

When young, grass internodes are short and the blades sit close to each other. The culms continue to have short internodes at their base, but towards the apex of the plant, the culms stretch out as they reach maturity.

Normally branches only emerge from the base, from buds in the

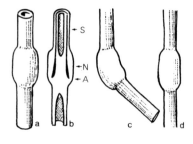

The node of a grass stem or culm, as seen from the outside (a) *and cut longitudinally* (b). *The culm is hollow except at the node. The leaf is attached at* (A). *Its base is swollen and forms the node* (N). *Thereafter, the blade invests the culm with a thin sheath* (S).

On erect culms the node is uniform all the way around (d), *but should the culm be knocked over by rain or wind it can right itself by growing more strongly on one side of the node* (c).

leaf-axils within the sheath. These buds continue to form new blades when the old ones have been cut off by mowing machines or grass-eating animals. In addition, new side buds are formed within the axils of the old shoots which is the main reason why when a lawn is mown regularly, the closer it becomes.

The secret of grass insensitivity to the scythe and grazing animals is that the growing points from which grass shoots emerge continue to be at ground level until just before the plant comes into flower. In annuals, the shoots die down when the plants reach maturity. In perennial grasses, by contrast, new side shoots emerge from the underground stems or rhizomes. Usually the aerial parts of the culm are not branched but amongst our indigenous grasses the Reed Canary Grass (3) and Purple Small-Reed (16), send out side shoots from blades higher up the culm.

In grass species indigenous to the British Isles perennial growth occurs in several different ways. For example, in grasses with vertical stolons and tuftlike growth such as Cocksfoot (36), the lateral shoots only have very short underground portions. Normally the sheaths, containing the rapidly developing lateral shoots, quickly split and die, and the withered membranes remain to protect the new shoots. In grasses with creeping stolons and upright culms the side shoots grow horizontally underground before they emerge out of the ground. A good example of this is Couch Grass

A grass flower (Bread Wheat, 81)–(a) without the palea and lemma or flowering glumes and (b) with them. On the right, the palea (P) and lemma (L) as seen from the dorsal side. In front of the pistil (PI) are two lodicules (LO), which, during flowering, move away from each other. The pistil has two styles (S), which culminate in long hairy stigmas. The three stamens (A) have large, rocking anthers and thin filaments, which are attached to the centre of the anther.

(76). Other species send out lateral shoots which grow horizontally along the ground and develop roots at the nodes before emerging from the surface (e.g. Creeping Bent, 14). Grass roots are adventitious and they spread out in a tight bundle from any section or part of the stem to be found under or just above the ground during growth. The seedling radicle withers very quickly.

With annual grasses it is normal for all shoots to reach maturity before they die. By contrast, perennial grasses produce vegetative shoots which branch out from the vertical stems or stolons. Normally these vegetative shoots are rather shorter and their blades are more tightly bunched together than those of the fertile shoots. Sometimes, grasses with horizontal, creeping rhizomes (e.g. Couch Grass, 76) form vegetative shoots during the summer which can reach nearly the same height as the flowering culms. The upright vegetative shoots of Couch and various other grasses such as the Wood Melick (38) however, die down during the winter and the buds lie hidden underground. The majority of the other perennial grasses remain green throughout the winter and have their buds situated at ground level. They are capable of producing and growing new leaves throughout the year except when the cold weather stops their growth. The older, fully-developed leaves die down in the winter, of course, but they persist as a protective covering for the fresh, young shoots.

Because of their propensity for survival it is not surprising that grasses form one of the most dominant forms of natural vegetation which covers the surface of the Earth.

Flowers and Fruits of Grasses

As mentioned before, grass flowers are small and inconspicuous. Actually, in many species they are so small that it is necessary to use a magnifying glass to study them. It is also advisable to have a pair of pointed tweezers and a couple of needles handy during identification to help separate the various spikelet parts – a job which requires both patience and practice.

The true flower of a grass consists of the stamens, the stigmas and ovary and two small scales, the lodicules. As a rule there are only three stamens, but in some tropical species of grass, e.g. Bamboo

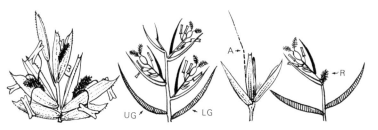

On the left a three-flowered spikelet of Bread Wheat (81). In the diagram, there are two glumes, the lower glume (LG) and the upper glume (UG). The lemma is left white like the axis of the spikelet, and the palea has been coloured black. The axis of the spikelet culminates in a sterile flower, which is represented only by the lemma and palea.

On the right, is a one-flowered spikelet of another species of grass, Narrow Small-Reed (17). In this species, the lemma is invested with an awn (A), which protrudes from the dorsal surface. The axis of the spikelet culminates in a short stem, the so-called rachilla (R), which is covered with long hairs.

and Rice, there can be six stamens and in a couple of British species, there are fewer than three, i.e. the Sweet Vernal Grass (1), which has two stamens and the Squirrel-Tail Fescue (59) which has just one.

Each stamen has a thin stalk, the filament, which bears a large wind-pollinated anther. Being wind-pollinated, pollen from the anther is produced in copious amounts. It is a well known fact that the presence of grass-pollen in the air can cause great discomfort to many people who are allergic to pollen wall proteins; to the extent that they suffer from hay-fever at mid-summer. To take Rye as an example, it has been calculated that each anther contains about 19,000 pollen grains. Each ear of rye comprises at least seventy flowers each with three stamens, thus producing about four million pollen grains. It is impossible to calculate how many are produced by a whole field of rye. For effective cross-pollination to be achieved in wind-pollinated plants, the pollen grain/embryo sac ratio is extremely high. The four million grains of pollen produced in an ear of rye correspond to about seventy female embryo sacs in the same ear. Thus, to ensure pollination of a single rye embryo, some

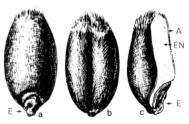

The fruit of a grass grain is a nut of a particular type in which the seed-coat has merged with the ovary wall. It is called a caryopsis. The illustration shows a grain of wheat (*81*) from the (a) dorsal, and (b) the ventral side, and (c) a longi-tudinal section.

The embryo (E) is small and lies obliquely at the base of the fruit. The rest of the fruit consists of carbohydrate-rich endosperm (EN) and just below the seed-coat is a layer consisting of large endosperm cells (A) the aleurone cells, which are particularly rich in albumin and vitamins.

The embryo (E) can be seen from the surface of the seed-coat as a small impression at the base of the dorsal side of the fruit (a). On the ventral side (b) there is a deep groove, the ventral suture, which varies in depth in different species.

57,000 pollen grains are produced.

The pistil or gynoecium consists of an ovary, a style and a stigma. The ovary has a single locus seed chamber at the base and usually three styles with feathery stigmas situated at the top. The stigmas dangle out of the flower at anthesis and are well-suited for catching wind-borne pollen. Naturally pollen from different plant species fall onto the hairs of the stigma, but only those grains of pollen which are compatible with the stigmas are able to penetrate and grow down through the styles to fertilise the embryo in the ovary.

Sometimes the pollen grain which fertilises the egg does not actually belong to the same species as the mother plant, but to a closely related species. Thus, occasional interspecific hybrids are produced by cross fertilisation. Most hybrids cannot produce viable seeds. However, under certain conditions, particularly when polyploids are produced by the doubling of the chromosomes in the germ cells of the hybrid plant, the hybrid can exist as a new species with fertile seed production. A good example is Townsend's Cord-Grass (*92*).

The true flower is surrounded by two scales, the lemma and palea. The membranous scale investing the embryo is called the palea and the lower more herbaceous scale is called the lemma. During anthesis, the lodicules prise open the lemma and palea, so that the anthers and stigmas become exposed. After flowering the lodicules wither away and the scales close up again.

Some grasses, for example, the Sweet Vernal Grass (1) and the Marsh or Floating Fox-Tail (10) have no lodicules, so the anthers and stigmas have to emerge on their own. These grasses are proto-gynous, a condition in which the stigmas appear first and when they have faded the anthers then appear. Usually in grasses with lodicules the stigmas and anthers appear simultaneously. Self-pollination is therefore theoretically possible, but is usually pre-vented by a self-incompatibility system. Outcrossing is normally the rule for most species of grass but there are a number which are self-compatible. Several species of grass are capable of producing viable seeds parthenogenetically without fertilisation at all, by a mechanism known as apomixis.

The single florets are assembled in aggregations known as spike-lets, whereby several of them are surrounded by two larger scales, the glumes. The glumes themselves represent the base of the spikelet and are arranged in alternate rows, or pairs, along the axis of the inflorescence. Usually there are two glumes, the upper and the

The composite inflorescences in grasses are called panicles (a), *when the single spikelets are placed at some distance from each other on long branches* (e.g. *Meadow-Grass, 44*). *The spike-like inflorescences are called racemes* (b *and* c) *when the spikelets are placed close together on quite short stalks* (e.g. *Sweet Vernal Grass, 1, and Meadow or Common Fox-Tail, 69*) *or if the spikelets are placed directly on the axis of the inflorescence* (d) (e.g. *Hybrid Sea-Couch*). *It is possible to find clusters of spikes* (e) (e.g. *Smooth Finger-Grass, 88*) *when the inflorescences are composed of several spikes or spike-like inflorescences.*

lower glume respectively. No florets are found in the lower glume, but the upper glume contains one or more florets or flowering sideshoots.

The complete flower then consists of two glumes, a lemma, a palea, two lodicules, one to three anthers, one to three stigmas and styles, and an ovary. The glumes, which in fact are modified bracts, substitute for the missing leaves of the perianth.

In many species of grass, the palea tightly invests the ripe seed and the lemma of the flower is often supplied with a bristle-shaped growth, an awn, which can have significance during seed dispersal. At maturity, the rhachis falls to pieces. Often a little piece of the rhachis remains attached to the seed, together with the lemma and palea. The mature diaspore of grasses is a very specialised type of fruit, known as a caryopis in which the seed wall, the testa, is fused with the walls of the ovary. In some grasses such as rye and wheat, the grains are 'naked' in that they are not invested by the lemma and palea at maturity. In others, the grain is more or less tightly invested by the lemma and palea, and sometimes completely amalgamated as in barley. The grain often has a longitudinal groove known as the hilum. Inside the testa or seed coat, the grain consists of two parts, a carbohydrate rich endosperm and an embryo. The latter is the young grass plant at an immature stage and occurs at the base of the grain. It is the energy-rich endosperm which nourishes the embryo during germination which has made cereal grasses such as wheat and rice important staple crops to man.

When the grains germinate, enzymes are produced by the embryo which convert the insoluble starches of the endosperm into soluble sugars which are absorbed as nourishment by the embryo. The brewing industry uses this ability of the grass embryo to convert insoluble starches into soluble sugars, when barley is converted into malt in the first stage of the beer brewing process. This sugar-rich malt extract, known as wort, is fermented with yeast to produce beer.

The number of fertile flowers in a spikelet is very variable, ranging from many down to two or even only one. At times evidence of reduction can be observed in that one also finds sterile rudiments of other florets by the presence of barren lemmas, etc.

Spikelets are grouped together in inflorescences of varying shapes and sizes but particularly in panicles, racemes or spikes.

When the individual spikelets are borne on stalks on branches from the main axis, the inflorescence is a panicle (e.g. Tall Oat-Grass, 26). On the left is a panicle which has already flowered, and to the right a panicle in full bloom.

When the spikelets are borne on stalks emerging directly from the main axis the inflorescence is a raceme, e.g. *Brachypodium* (67). When there are no stalks, and the spikelets are arranged directly onto the main axis, the inflorescence is known as a spike. The spikelets may be arranged alternately around the stem or alternately in two rows, which gives the axis an appearance of being sinuated or jointed. Most commonly only one spikelet is found at each joint, as in, for example, the Perennial Rye-Grass (77) and Couch Grass (76), although sometimes two or three can be found at each node as in Lyme Grass (69).

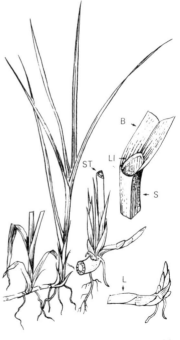

Sedges are perennial herbs and their shoots grow from buds on the stolons. In the illustration (Carnation Sedge, 134), the stolons have horizontal, creeping runners, so that the shoots emerge at intervals.

In other species the stolon can have vertical growth so as to produce tufts. The stolon is invested in a membranous scale leaf (L).

The lower leaves on the upright shoot consist solely of sheaths. The upper leaves have sheaths (S) and long, narrow blades (B). The sheath forms a closed tube (with no free edge), unless it happens to burst as the shoot emerges, which is often the case as far as the lower sheaths are concerned. At the junction of the sheath and blade, a short ligule (LI) is to be seen.

The shoots can easily be identified by the fact that the leaves are placed in three rows up the triangular pith-filled stem (ST).

The Sedge Family

Plants of the Sedge family (Cyperaceae) superficially look very like the 'true' grasses, and like them have inconspicuous greenish or brownish wind-pollinated flowers. Sedges are easily distinguished from grasses however, by their nodeless, pith-filled culms which are triangular in cross-section and leaf blades that are arranged in three rows on the shoots. In Grasses the stems are usually hollow and terete and have nodes, and the leaves are always arranged in two rows. Another major difference is that in sedges the bracts which subtend the spikelets are nearly always leaf-like, whereas in the grasses they are never leaf-like. The growth habit is similar to that of grasses in that cell division occurs at the nodes of the stem-base which are protected by the surrounding leaf-sheaths. Unlike grasses, which have open sheaths, the culms of sedges are invested with closed leaf-sheaths.

The leaves have a long, linear-shaped blade and these have, as a

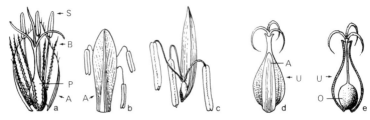

The sedge flower emerges from the axil of the glume-like bracts (A). In some species the flowers are bisexual and they are often equipped with hairs or bristles (B) as shown in fig. a, the Wood Club-Rush (101). These bristles may be considered to be a strongly reduced perianth.

As a rule, there are three stamens (S) with upright or nodding anthers attached by their bases to their filaments.

The pistil (P) has an ovary and a style, divided into two or three stigmas.

In Carex (b–e), the flower is invariably unisexual. A male flower seen from the dorsal side (b) and from the ventral side (c). The female flower is surrounded by a bottle-shaped utricle (U), through which the pointed stigmas emerge. The female flower with its utricle is illustrated from the dorsal side of the glume (d) and a cross-section of the utricle is illustrated (e) so that the ovary (O) can be seen.

Sedge flowers are usually in spikes or spike-like inflorescences which, in some species, are placed singly at the top of the stems and in others are grouped in composite inflorescences. The inflorescence is subtended from the base by a bract.

The Common Spike-Rush (97) has an upright spike (a). At the base it is surrounded by two sterile glumes, but all the others support bisexual flowers.

The other three figures show composite spikes of various species of Carex. *The panicle of the Remote Sedge (117) (b) has male flowers below (each with three anthers) and female flowers above (each with two stigmas).*

The composite inflorescence of the Sand Sedge (112) consists of several identical panicles (c), each of which can contain both male and female flowers.

The composite inflorescence of Carnation Sedge (134) has a small terminal spike containing solely male flowers and below that two spike-like inflorescences consisting entirely of female flowers (d).

rule, only a small ligule at the transition between the sheath and the blade. In some sedges, the blade is flat, or folded lengthwise, in others it can be gully-shaped, semi-circular, triangular or bristle-like.

Sedges are perennial herbs with stolons which bear sheath-like scale-leaves. In some sedges the stolon is perpendicular and branches upwards, so that the plant forms a close tufted growth. Others have horizontal, creeping stolons from which upright shoots are formed; these can either be prostate and spread out, or in close tufts. Being perennials, vegetative shoots are produced in addition to the flowering shoots.

Sedges normally grow in damp, boggy places where sometimes they can dominate the whole vegetation. They play an important role in nature at the edges of streams and lakes in the formation of turf and overgrowth. They have little value for animal fodder as their leaves and culms are usually stiff and sharp on account of siliceous cells which occur in them.

In the Cyperaceae, the tiny flowers can either be hermaphrodite or more usually, as in the genus *Carex*, the true sedges, unisexual where males are separate from the females. The flowers arise from the base or axil of a glume and are arranged into single- or many-flowered spikelets. The spikelets can be solitary, terminal or grouped into a branched or spike-like inflorescence and occasionally grouped into composite inflorescences. In most species true perianth tissue is totally lacking but in some of the more primitive members of the family, traces of perianth can be seen in the form of bristles or hairs. A good example is the cotton grass genus *Eriophorum* (106, 107). The glume-like perianth of grasses is never really to be seen in sedges. By contrast, a subtending leaf-bract is usually found at the base of the inflorescence axis, which is more or less identical to the leaves. There are usually two or three stamens (more rarely one or six) in the male flower which are characterised by the basi-fixed anthers rather than medi-fixed (as in grasses). In the true sedges the female flowers consist basically of a bottle-shape utricle (flask) containing a single ovary and subtended by a glume. Within the utricle is an ovary which either has two stigmas and is a flat circular disc maturing into an ellipsoid bi-convex nut, or has three stigmas and is usually cylindrical maturing into a trigonous, ellipsoid or obovoid nut. Unlike the grasses the testa of the sedge seed is not coalesced with the walls of the ovary to produce a caryopsis.

Seed dispersal is often accomplished by the aid of animals, wind and water. For instance, the seeds of Cotton-Grass (106, 107) are sent far afield with the help of the wind. The thorns of the perianth-bristles on the white Beak Sedge, *Rhyncospora alba* (95), catch in the fleece of animals, and the spongy seed-wall of Saw Sedge, *Cladium mariscus* (105) make it possible for the fruits to float and persist in water for some time.

The sedge family consists of about 100 genera with a total of about 4,000 species in the world, and in the British Isles, twelve genera are represented by about ninety species, two thirds belonging to the genus *Carex*.

The Rush Family

By contrast to both the grasses and the sedges, plants belonging to the Rush family (Juncaceae) have completely developed flowers with two dry, glume-like perianth whorls. Their basic morphology, if studied in detail, is seen to be identical to that of the flowers of, for example, the Lily family.

The flowers of the Rush family are wind-pollinated and thus their sepals and petals are not so spectacular as their insect-pollinated relatives.

The regular flowers are hypogynous with six perianth leaves in two whorls. Normally there are six stamens also arranged in two whorls, although sometimes the inner whorl is absent, so that the flower has only three stamens. The anthers are basi-fixed just as in sedges, and not medi-fixed as in grasses. In the gynoecium, there is a central style with a column culminating in three stigmas, corresponding to the three carpels of the ovary. The fruit is a capsule with few, or many seeds, the endosperms of which are rich in carbohydrates. The persistant perianth remains attached to the fruit at maturity. In Rushes the seed dispersal is by animals, when the seed-pod becomes sticky and the seeds are damp at maturity. Species of woodrush have a juicy, oil-rich appendage to the seeds

Plants belonging to the Rush family have fully developed trimerous flowers with two whorls of dry, glume-like perianth leaves (P), two whorls of stamens (S) (or rarely one) and a central pistil which consists of a tri-carpellate ovary and a style with three stigmas (ST).

The fruit is a capsule (b), which at maturity is surrounded by a persistent perianth. Eventually the capsule opens by three valves (c). The base of the perianth is surrounded by membranous bracts (B).

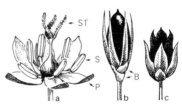

Inflorescences of the Rush family. The flowers can be either placed singly in an open tassel-like inflorescence, as in (a) Hairy Woodrush (145), or they can be grouped into tight clusters, which are also arranged in tassel-like inflorescences, for example (b) Jointed Rush (142) and (c) Many-Flowered Woodrush (147). Bracts occur at the base of the inflorescence.

which is considered to be an attractant for dispersal by ants.

There are various types of inflorescences in the Rush family. At one extreme, the flowers are grouped together in open tassel-shaped inflorescences known as cymes, e.g. *Juncus effusus* (138), where the flowers occur singly on the branches. At the other extreme the flowers occur in head-shaped inflorescences, e.g. *Luzula campestris* (146) which are grouped into larger, denser panicles. Usually small glume-like bracteoles appear at the base of each flower and a similar leaf-like bract, at the base of the inflorescence.

All British species are annual or perennial grass-like herbs with cylindrical (seldom compressed), pith-filled culms without nodes. In some species of rush, the pith of the culm has distinct air-pockets. The culms are invested by the leaf-sheaths.

The leaf blades are narrow and linear and they can either be flat, channelled (with turned up edges) or absolutely cylindrical (with a circular cross-section). A small ligule usually develops at the transition between the sheath and the blade. The leaves are usually placed in three rows on the stem as in sedges.

The family consists in all of nine genera with about 400 species occurring in temperate regions throughout the world. The majority of them belong to the genera *Juncus* and *Luzula*, the Rushes and Woodrushes, as they do in the British Isles where these genera are represented by about twenty species.

1 **Sweet Vernal Grass**
Anthoxanthum odoratum

2 **Holy Grass**
Hierochloe odorata

3 **Reed Canary Grass**
Phalaris arundinacea

1

2

3

4

5

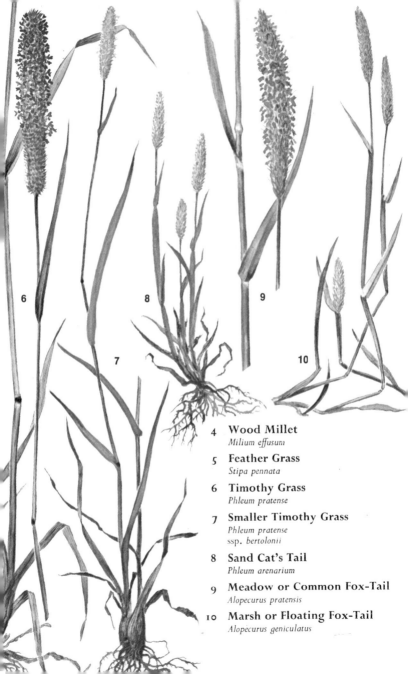

4 **Wood Millet**
Milium effusum

5 **Feather Grass**
Stipa pennata

6 **Timothy Grass**
Phleum pratense

7 **Smaller Timothy Grass**
Phleum pratense
ssp. *bertolonii*

8 **Sand Cat's Tail**
Phleum arenarium

9 **Meadow or Common Fox-Tail**
Alopecurus pratensis

10 **Marsh or Floating Fox-Tail**
Alopecurus geniculatus

11

12

13

14

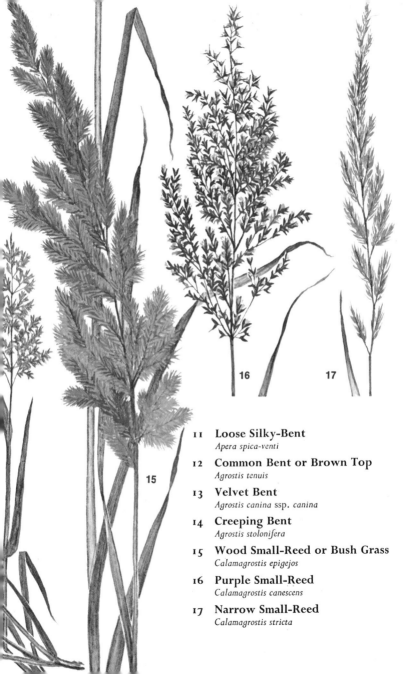

11 **Loose Silky-Bent**
Apera spica-venti

12 **Common Bent or Brown Top**
Agrostis tenuis

13 **Velvet Bent**
Agrostis canina ssp. *canina*

14 **Creeping Bent**
Agrostis stolonifera

15 **Wood Small-Reed or Bush Grass**
Calamagrostis epigejos

16 **Purple Small-Reed**
Calamagrostis canescens

17 **Narrow Small-Reed**
Calamagrostis stricta

18

19

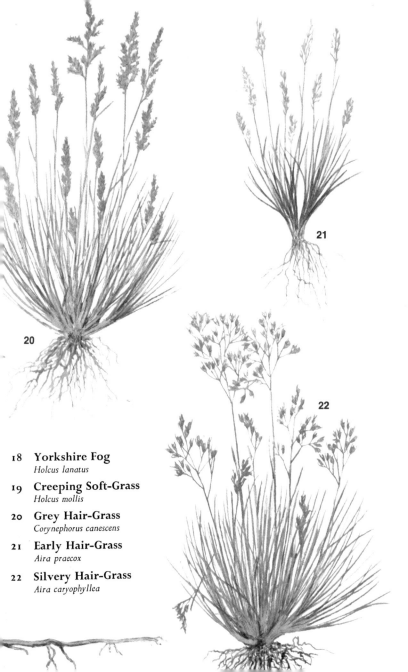

18 **Yorkshire Fog**
   Holcus lanatus

19 **Creeping Soft-Grass**
   Holcus mollis

20 **Grey Hair-Grass**
   Corynephorus canescens

21 **Early Hair-Grass**
   Aira praecox

22 **Silvery Hair-Grass**
   Aira caryophyllea

23 **Tufted Hair-Grass**
Deschampsia caespitosa

24 **Wavy Hair-Grass**
Deschampsia flexuosa

25 **Yellow or Golden Oat-Grass**
Trisetum flavescens

26 **Tall Oat-Grass**
Arrhenatherum elatius

23

24

25   26

27   28

27 **Meadow Oat-Grass**
Avenula pratensis

28 **Hairy Oat-Grass**
Avenula pubescens

29 **Common Reed-Grass**
Phragmites australis

30 **Purple Moor-Grass**
Molinia caerulea

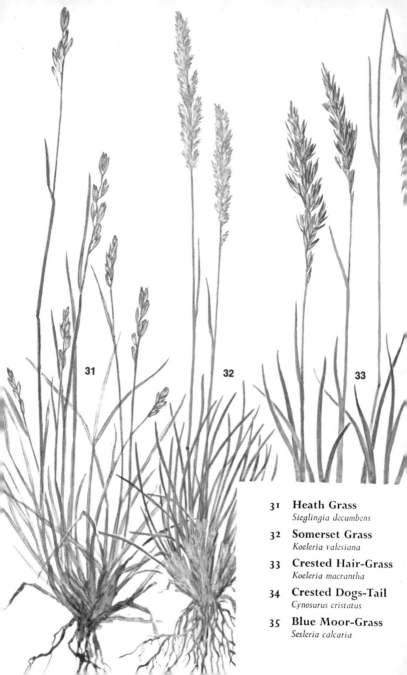

31 **Heath Grass**
   Sieglingia decumbens

32 **Somerset Grass**
   Koeleria valesiana

33 **Crested Hair-Grass**
   Koeleria macrantha

34 **Crested Dogs-Tail**
   Cynosurus cristatus

35 **Blue Moor-Grass**
   Sesleria calcaria

34

35

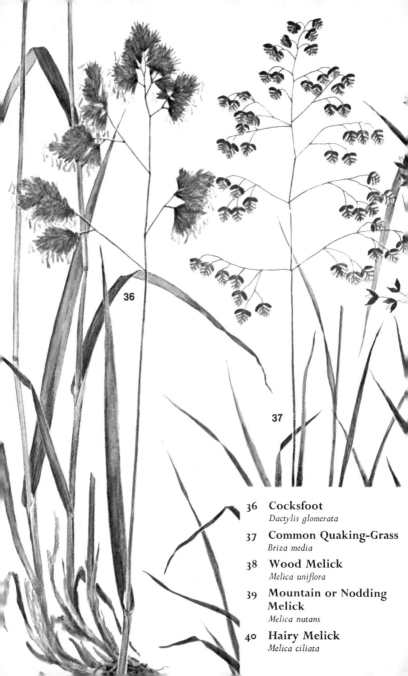

36 **Cocksfoot**
Dactylis glomerata

37 **Common Quaking-Grass**
Briza media

38 **Wood Melick**
Melica uniflora

39 **Mountain or Nodding Melick**
Melica nutans

40 **Hairy Melick**
Melica ciliata

38   39   40

41 **Water Whorl-Grass**
   Catabrosa aquatica

42 **Love Grass**
   Eragrostis minor

43 **Annual Meadow-Grass**
   Poa annua

44 **Smooth Meadow-Grass**
   Poa pratensis

45 **Rough Meadow-Grass**
   Poa trivialis

44

45

46   47   48

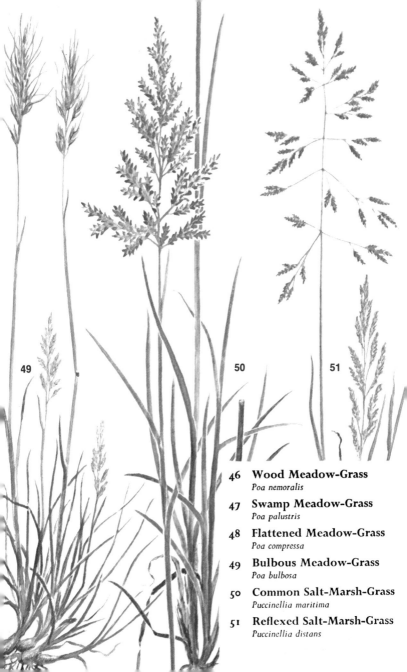

46 Wood Meadow-Grass
Poa nemoralis

47 Swamp Meadow-Grass
Poa palustris

48 Flattened Meadow-Grass
Poa compressa

49 Bulbous Meadow-Grass
Poa bulbosa

50 Common Salt-Marsh-Grass
Puccinellia maritima

51 Reflexed Salt-Marsh-Grass
Puccinellia distans

52

53

52 **Reed Sweet-Grass**
    Glyceria maxima

53 **Floating Sweet-Grass**
    Glyceria fluitans

54 **Giant Fescue**
    Festuca gigantea

55 **Meadow Fescue**
    Festuca pratensis

56 **Tall Fescue**
    Festuca arundinacea

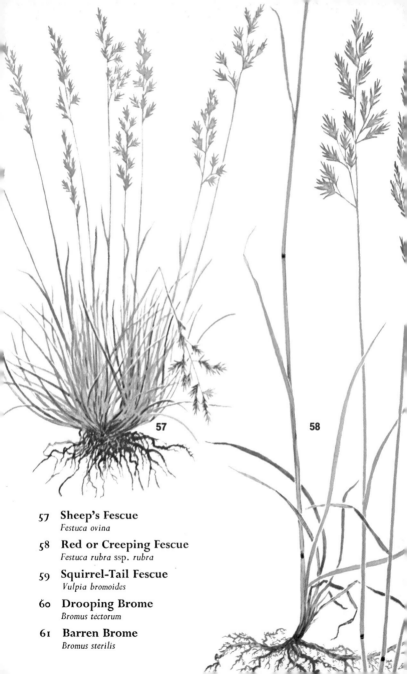

57 **Sheep's Fescue**
Festuca ovina

58 **Red or Creeping Fescue**
Festuca rubra ssp. *rubra*

59 **Squirrel-Tail Fescue**
Vulpia bromoides

60 **Drooping Brome**
Bromus tectorum

61 **Barren Brome**
Bromus sterilis

59   60   61

62

63

64

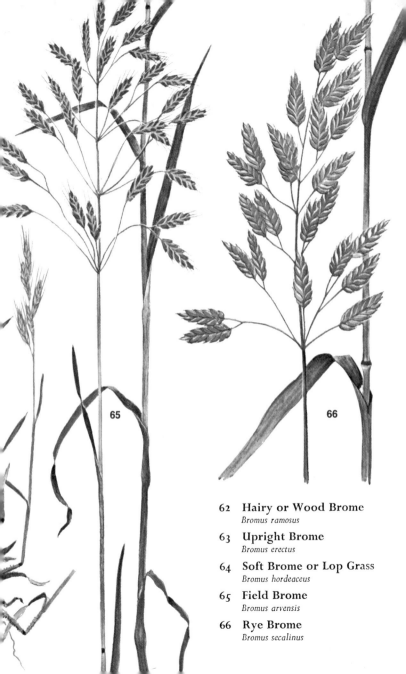

65

66

62 **Hairy or Wood Brome**
    Bromus ramosus

63 **Upright Brome**
    Bromus erectus

64 **Soft Brome or Lop Grass**
    Bromus hordeaceus

65 **Field Brome**
    Bromus arvensis

66 **Rye Brome**
    Bromus secalinus

67

68

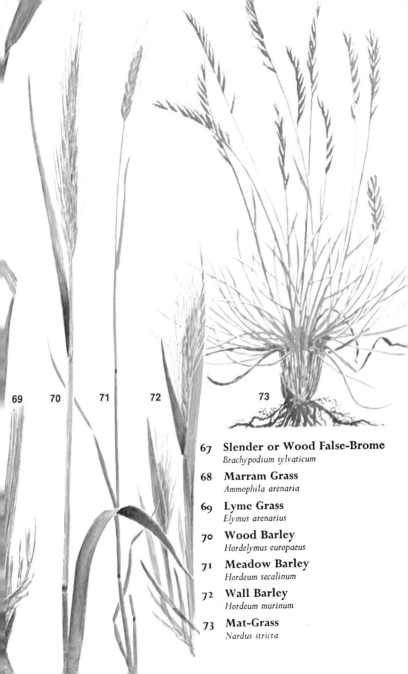

67   **Slender or Wood False-Brome**
Brachypodium sylvaticum

68   **Marram Grass**
Ammophila arenaria

69   **Lyme Grass**
Elymus arenarius

70   **Wood Barley**
Hordelymus europaeus

71   **Meadow Barley**
Hordeum secalinum

72   **Wall Barley**
Hordeum murinum

73   **Mat-Grass**
Nardus stricta

74 75 76

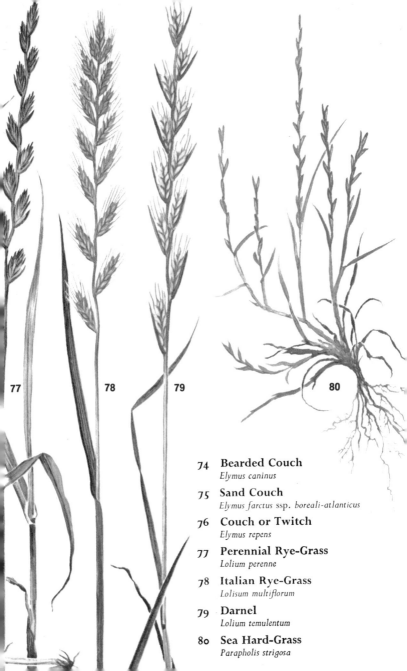

74 **Bearded Couch**
Elymus caninus

75 **Sand Couch**
Elymus farctus ssp. *boreali-atlanticus*

76 **Couch or Twitch**
Elymus repens

77 **Perennial Rye-Grass**
Lolium perenne

78 **Italian Rye-Grass**
Lolisum multiflorum

79 **Darnel**
Lolium temulentum

80 **Sea Hard-Grass**
Parapholis strigosa

81 **Bread Wheat**
Triticum aestivum

82 **Rye**
Secale cereale

83 **Two-Rowed Barley**
Hordeum distichon

84 **Six-Rowed Barley**
Hordeum vulgare

85 **Oats**
Avena sativa

86 **Bristol or Small Oat**
Avena fatua

85

86

87

88

89

87 Common or Broom-Corn Millet
Panicum miliaceum

88 Smooth Finger-Grass
Digitaria ischaemum

89 Cockspur Grass
Echinochloa crus-galli

90 Green Bristle-Grass
Setaria viridis

91 Italian Millet or Fox-Tail
Setaria italica

92 Townsend's Cord-Grass
Spartina townsendii

93   94   95

96 97 98 99 100

101

102

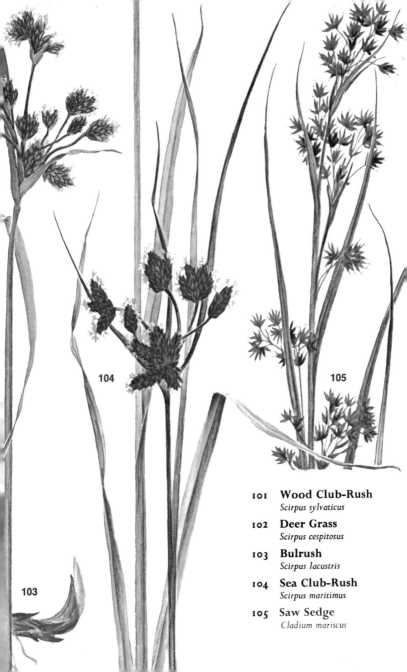

101	**Wood Club-Rush** *Scirpus sylvaticus*
102	**Deer Grass** *Scirpus cespitosus*
103	**Bulrush** *Scirpus lacustris*
104	**Sea Club-Rush** *Scirpus maritimus*
105	**Saw Sedge** *Cladium mariscus*

106　　　　107　　　108

113 114 115 116

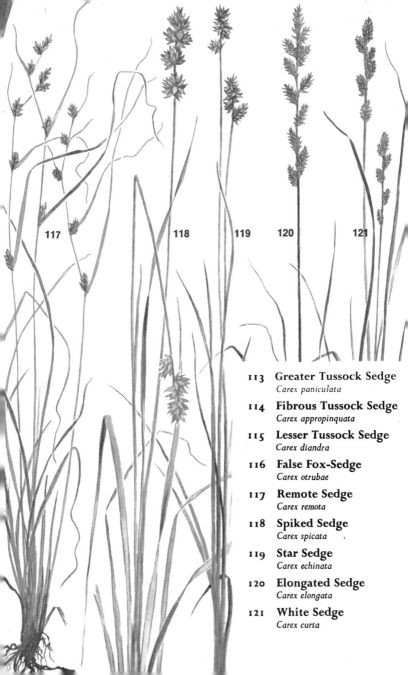

113 **Greater Tussock Sedge**
Carex paniculata

114 **Fibrous Tussock Sedge**
Carex appropinquata

115 **Lesser Tussock Sedge**
Carex diandra

116 **False Fox-Sedge**
Carex otrubae

117 **Remote Sedge**
Carex remota

118 **Spiked Sedge**
Carex spicata

119 **Star Sedge**
Carex echinata

120 **Elongated Sedge**
Carex elongata

121 **White Sedge**
Carex curta

122   123   124   125

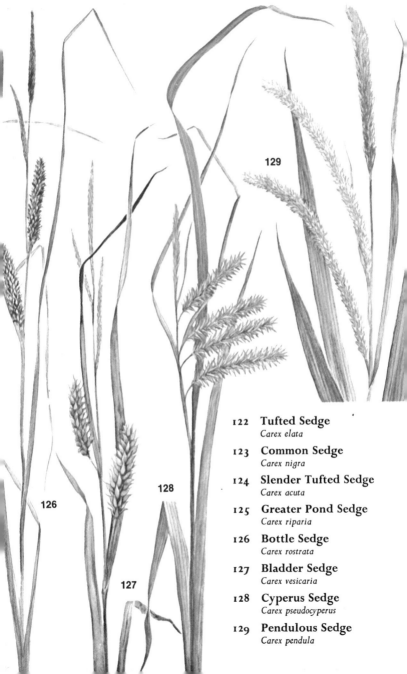

126

129

128

127

122 **Tufted Sedge**
Carex elata

123 **Common Sedge**
Carex nigra

124 **Slender Tufted Sedge**
Carex acuta

125 **Greater Pond Sedge**
Carex riparia

126 **Bottle Sedge**
Carex rostrata

127 **Bladder Sedge**
Carex vesicaria

128 **Cyperus Sedge**
Carex pseudocyperus

129 **Pendulous Sedge**
Carex pendula

130   131   132   133

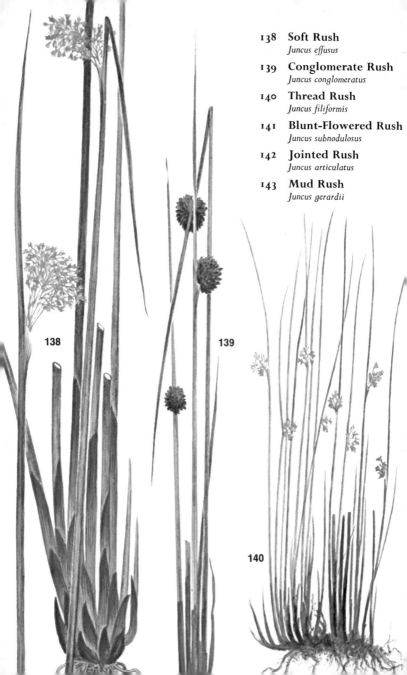

141

142

143

144 **Greater Woodrush**
Luzula sylvatica

145 **Hairy Woodrush**
Luzula pilosa

146 **Field Woodrush**
Luzula campestris

147 **Many-Flowered Woodrush**
Luzula multiflora

DESCRIPTION OF THE SPECIES

THE GRASS FAMILY – GRAMINEAE

1 Sweet Vernal Grass
Anthoxanthum odoratum

A perennial growing in dense tufts; culms slender, 10–100 cm long. The leaves are fairly short with narrow blades with long, dense hairs at the base; the ligule is of medium length, 1–5 mm. The inflorescence is a long green or purplish panicle made up of narrow, somewhat compressed spikelets. Each spikelet contains a single hermaphrodite, viable floret, surrounded by two sterile florets. The sterile florets consist simply of rust-brown awned hairy lemmas. The lemma of the fertile floret is smooth and has no awn. In contrast to most other grasses, the viable floret of Sweet Vernal Grass has only two stamens. The florets are protogynous; the long feather-shaped stigmas emerging from the spikelets before the stamens. Flowering period: late April to July.

The ripe caryopsis is tightly enclosed in the shiny reddish-

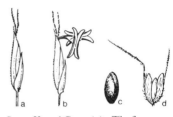

Sweet Vernal Grass (1). The flowers are protogynous – (a) spikelet at the female stage with protruding stigmas, (b) spikelet at the male phase with emerging anthers, (c) a ripe seed surrounded by the awnless fertile lemma, (d) floret with awned lemmas. (a and b: 2 × , c and d: 3 × natural size.)

brown lemma and palea. These are surrounded by the hairy, awned lemmas of the sterile florets, and are believed to function as an aid to seed dispersal. At maturity the panicle becomes yellowish in colour. The plant contains coumarin which gives the hay a characteristic spicy scent. It has no great value as fodder partly because of low productivity and partly because of the bitter taste of coumarin.

Sweet Vernal Grass is common throughout the British Isles both in meadows and uncultivated dry commons, open woodlands and especially in sandy soil and also is widespread in Europe and Asia.

2 Holy Grass
Hierochloe odorata

Perennial with creeping rhizomes and numerous sterile shoots; culms 20–50 cm long, erect. The leaves of the sterile shoots are long, those on the flowering culms much shorter; the ligules are long. Panicle spreading with shiny brown spikelets. The spikelets have a hermaphrodite central floret, and two lateral male florets. The glumes are membranous. The male florets have two

Holy Grass (2) – (a) spikelet at the beginning of the flowering period, (b) the spikelet at a later stage with the glumes wide apart, so that each floret has become separated from the other, (4 × natural size.)

stamens, the hermaphrodite floret has three stamens. Flowering period: end of March to May.

This species contains coumarin and in the past, it was strewn at church doors on Holy Days so that the fragrance would scent the air. It grows in damp meadows and at the edges of ponds and streams. It is a rare grass in the British Isles, but widespread on both sides of the Atlantic and can be found in north-west Europe, eastern districts of North America and in Greenland.

3 Reed Canary Grass
Phalaris arundinacea

Perennial with creeping rhizomes; culms erect, up to 2 metres long, grey-green, sometimes branched. The leaves are long, broad and rough on both sides; the ligule is 2·5–16 mm long, white, becoming torn. Panicle large, lobate, blue-green or purple-red; the branches during flowering may be spreading or contracted against the axis. The spikelet has a single hermaphrodite floret. The glumes are as long as the spikelet. There are two narrow sterile lemmas, one on either side of the broad fertile

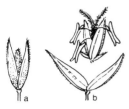

Reed Canary Grass (3) – (a) *a complete spikelet*, (b) *a dissected flowering spikelet showing the barren florets as two small scales at the base of the glumes of the fertile floret*, (c) *a ripe seed enveloped in the palea and the small sterile lemmas.* (*3 × natural size.*)

lemma; all three lemmas and the palea are enclosed by the glumes. Flowering period: June to August.

Reed Canary Grass forms dense stands in marshes at the edges of rivers, lakes, streams and ponds, and can be found in damp meadows. When young, it is eaten by grazing animals, but when mature, it becomes too coarse, but has been used for thatching. A variety of Reed Canary Grass with variegated leaves is grown as an ornamental. The grass is common throughout the British Isles and over the whole of the Northern Hemisphere.

4 Wood Millet
Milium effusum

Perennial forming loose tufts;

culms 45–180 cm long. The fresh green leaves are broad and floppy with rough edges; the ligules are long. The panicle is large with pale green spikelets on thread-like, spreading branches. The spikelets are ovate and have convex glumes the same length as, or slightly longer than, the lemma. The mature caryopsis is tightly enclosed by the shiny, greyish-brown cartilaginous, hard lemma and palea. Flowering period: May to July.

It is a characteristic woodland grass, which is found especially in humus-rich soil. In established open Beech woods it can cover large areas. It is widespread over most of the British Isles where there is suitable woodland soil. It is also found in the temperate zones of the Northern Hemisphere.

Wood Millet (4) – (a) *a flowering spikelet*, (b) *a mature spikelet*, (c) *a ripe seed enveloped in the shiny, hard palea.* (*4 × natural size.*)

5 Feather Grass
Stipa pennata

A blue-green perennial growing in dense tufts; culms 25–40 cms long, stiff, erect and smooth. The narrow inrolled leaves are bristle-shaped; the ligules are long and pointed. The inflorescence is a spreading feathery panicle. The spikelet has a single floret. The lemma has an awn up to 20 cm long, the upper $\frac{2}{3}$ bearing two rows of setae. When young, the inflorescence is enveloped by the sheath of the uppermost leaf and only the feathery awns protrude. At maturity it then becomes spreading. Flowering period: May to June.

A native of south-eastern Europe and central Asia, Feather Grass was introduced to gardens in Britain for its ornamental inflorescences.

CAT'S TAIL

Species of the Cat's Tail genus, *Phleum* can be recognised by their small, dense spike-like panicles, consisting of single-flowered stalkless spikelets whose needle-sharp glumes are longer than the awnless lemma. The ripe caryopsis is only loosely contained in the mebranous lemma from which it is easily separated.

The name 'Cat's Tail' refers to the inflorescence. The genus consists of twelve species of which five are found in the British Isles.

6 Timothy Grass
Phleum pratense

A tufted perennial; culms 40–150 cm long, erect and often a little swollen at the base. The pale green or bluish-green leaves are flat and fairly broad with rough edges; the ligules are rather long on the upper leaves, up to 6 mm. The panicle is dense, cylindrical, 6–15 cm long and 6–10 mm wide. The spikelets are flattened. The needle-sharp glumes are awned and keeled, the keels bearing stiff hairs. The lemma is membranous and has no awn. Flowering period: June to August.

Timothy Grass is one of our most important fodder grasses. It has been cultivated in the British Isles for at least 150

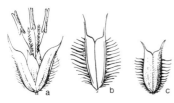

Flowering spikelet (a) *of Timothy Grass* (6) *with the glumes separated to show the lemma and* (b) *spikelet at maturity compared with* (c) *spikelet of Smaller Timothy Grass* (7). (4 × *natural size.*)

years. The seed is usually sown mixed with other grasses or clover.

The name Timothy Grass is derived from Timothy Hansen, who in the 1700's suggested it should be grown for fodder in the USA. It is now widespread both as a wild and cultivated species on both sides of the Atlantic and indeed over the whole of the Northern and part of the Southern Hemisphere. It is commonly found in meadows and roadsides but its original habitat was probably water meadows and low-lying grasslands.

7 Smaller Timothy Grass
Phleum pratense ssp. *bertolonii*

Perennial with long stolons; culms 6–70 cm long, slender with bulbous swellings at the base. The panicle is short and narrow, 1–8 cm long and 3–6 mm wide. Flowering period: July.

Smaller Timothy Grass looks like a diminutive form of Timothy Grass. It is commonly found growing on dry, grassy slopes and banks over most of the country. It is a hardy grass sometimes used for lawns and sports fields and to seed roadsides. It is widespread in Europe, the Near East and North Africa.

8 Sand Cat's Tail
Pleum arenarium

A closely tufted annual; culms usually 1–15 cm long. Leaves with inflated sheaths and very short blades. The panicle is small and club-shaped. Flowering period: May to July.

It is found scattered around the coast of the British Isles, on the dunes and cliffs, and is also widespread along the coasts of the Mediterranean and Baltic Seas.

FOX-TAIL

The inflorescence in species of the Fox-Tail genus *Alopecurus* is a dense cylindrical panicle, rounded at either end. The glumes are often united in their lower part. The lemma is shorter than the glumes with a long awn which protrudes from the spikelet.

The Fox-Tails can be distinguished from the Cat's Tails by the looser, softer panicles (hence the name Fox-Tail) and the united glumes. There are about fifty species, six occurring in the British Isles.

9 Meadow or Common Fox-Tail
Alopecurus pratensis

A tufted perennial, with numerous sterile leafy shoots; flowering culms, single or very few, 30–120 cm long. The leaves have flat broad blades; the ligules are truncate. The inflorescence is a dense, cylindrical panicle 2–13 cm long. The spikelets are 1–6 mm long, falling entire at maturity. Flowering period: mainly April to July, but can continue throughout the summer.

Meadow or Common Fox-Tail is a valuable fodder grass which requires rich, fertile soil. It grows in Britain and Europe and northern Asia, but is cultivated in many places throughout the world.

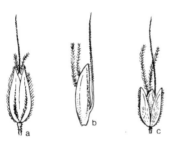

Flowering spikelet (a) of Meadow or Common Fox-Tail (9) at the female phase with emerging stigmas and (b) the fertile floret of the same species removed from the glumes, and surrounded by the awn-bearing lemma (the palea is absent). Spikelet (c) of Marsh or Floating Fox-Tail (10).(a: 3 ×, b and c: 4 × natural size.)

10 Marsh or Floating Fox-Tail
Alopecurus geniculatus

A tufted perennial, culms jointed, numerous, 15–45 cm long, creeping and root-forming at the nodes. The leaves have inflated sheaths and the uppermost blade is quite short; the ligule is long and somewhat

78

pointed. The dark green or purple tinged panicle is short and narrow. The spikelets are about 3 mm long excluding the long awns. Flowering period: June to August.

Marsh or Floating Fox-Tail grows in damp and often flooded soil at the edges of ditches and ponds. It is common throughout the British Isles and most of Europe.

Loose Silky Bent (11) – (a) spikelet and (b) seed shrouded by the palea and the lemma. The awn extends below the apex of the dorsal edge of the lemma. (5 × natural size.)

11 Loose Silky-Bent
Apera spica-venti

An annual; the culms 20–100 cm long; somewhat spreading. The leaves are narrow and rough; the ligules are long and fringed. The inflorescence is a large many-branched panicle up to 30 cm long with thin rough branches. The greenish- or reddish-purple tinged spikelets are single-flowered. The lemma has an awn 3–4 times its own length. Flowering period: June to early August.

Loose Silky-Bent is a very old field-weed which occurs on light, sandy soils, particularly in arable land. It is difficult to eradicate because the fine, light-weight seeds are produced in great quantities and may be blown miles away by the wind. The seeds ripen before the corn is harvested.

The origin of Loose Silky-Bent is uncertain, but the species is now widespread in cereal growing areas.

BENT

The Bent genus, *Agrostis* consists of 150–200 species of perennial grasses with thin, finely branched stems and panicles of compact single-flowered spikelets. The glumes are boat-shaped, membranous and longer than the lemmas and paleas. There are six species found in the British Isles.

12 Common Bent or Brown Top
Agrostis tenuis

Tuft-forming with short rhizomes; culms 10–70 cm long, slender. The leaves are flat; the ligule is short and blunt. The panicle is green or brownish-purple with branches spreading, even when mature. The lemma is usually without an awn. Flowering period: June to August.

Common Bent or Brown Top grows on poor, dry soil and can be found on commons, roadsides, scrubland and at the edges of woods and as a weed in hayfields, particularly on acid soils. It plays a major role as a fodder grass in natural pastures and is used for lawns and verges. It is a common native of the British Isles and throughout Europe and Asia. Through cultivation it has been accidentally introduced into North and South America, Australia, etc.

Common Bent may be distinguished from Velvet Bent and Brown Bent by the shorter, blunt ligule, the loose, open panicle and the usually awnless spikelets.

13 Velvet Bent
Agrostis canina ssp. *canina*

A blue-green perennial with creeping stolons producing loose tufts of bristle-shaped leaves; culms erect, 15–70 cm long. The leaves are flat; the ligules are long and pointed. The panicle is branched, delicate and somewhat loose during flowering, otherwise contracted. The spikelet is single-flowered. The lemma has a bent awn which protrudes from the

Common Bent or Brown Top (12) – (a) *flowering spikelet,* (b) *the same at maturity,* (c) *the fertile floret. Spikelet* (d) *of Velvet Bent (13) and* (e) *lemma of the same species. (8 × natural size.)*

spikelet. Flowering period: June
to August.

Velvet Bent grows in marshes
and in damp meadows with
poor soil. The species is widely
distributed throughout the
British Isles. It is also widespread in Europe, Asia and
north-east America.

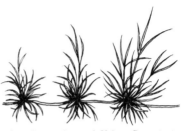

*Creeping stolons of Velvet Bent (13)
showing small tufts of vegetative shoots
with bristly inrolled leaves. (⅔ × natural
size.)*

14 Creeping Bent
Agrostis stolonifera

Loose tuft-forming perennial;
long rooting stolons; culms 10–
40 cm long, often bent at the
base. Leaves flat; ligules long.
Panicles delicate, branched,
open in flower, afterwards contracted, greenish-white or occasionally reddish. Spikelets
single-flowered. Lemmas
usually awnless, rarely with a
short awn near the tip. Flowering period: July and August.

Creeping Bent is common on
damp, rich soil both in fresh and
salt marshes. The species has
been cultivated for fodder,
especially in reclaimed areas
where it quickly forms a close
durable sward. It is no longer
used as a fodder grass, but the
seed is still used in lawn
mixtures. It was originally
indigenous to Europe and Asia,
but grows over most of the
world as a cultivated plant.

*Leaf ligules of (a) Common Bent or
Brown Top (12) and (b) Velvet Bent
(13). (4 × natural size.)*

SMALL-REED

The Small-Reed genus, *Calamagrostis* is comprised of robust perennial grasses with loose or dense panicles. The spikelets are narrow,
one-flowered with short pedicels which break up at maturity. The

81

awned lemma is shorter than the glumes, with a tuft of long, silky hairs at the base. The lemma and palea are membranous and enclose the mature caryopsis. There are about eighty species, of which four are British.

15 Wood Small-Reed or Bush Grass
Calamagrostis epigejos

A tough, greyish-green perennial with long rhizomes; culms 60–200 cm long, stiff, rough. The long, broad, rough leaves are inrolled in dry weather; the ligules are long and pointed, but later torn. The panicle is large, erect, densely-flowered and compact even during flowering. Flowering period: June to August.

Wood Small-Reed or Bush Grass grows in damp places, scrubland, at the edges of woods and roads, in ditches and fens, often forming pure stands. The species is common throughout the British Isles and widespread in Europe and eastern Asia. It forms hybrids with Marram Grass (68) giving Baltic Marram Grass, which is widely planted as a sand-binder.

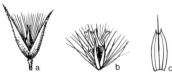

Wood Small-Reed or Bush Grass (15) – (a) spikelet (b) floret surrounded by the lemma, palea and with the outer glumes removed, and (c) inner side of lemma. (3 × natural size.)

16 Purple Small-Reed
Calamagrostis canescens

Perennial with horizontal, creeping rhizomes and numerous sterile leafy shoots; culms 60–120 cm long, fairly delicate, later branched. The leaves are long and narrow; the ligules are rather short. The panicle is large, soft and open during flowering but later compact. Flowering period: June and July.

Purple Small-Reed grows in large stands in damp meadows and waste ground. The species is fairly rare in the British Isles, but may be locally common. It is also found in central and northern Europe and western Siberia.

17 Narrow Small-Reed
Calamagrostis stricta

Perennial with slender creeping

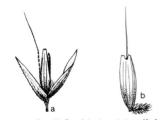

Narrow Small-Reed (17) – (a) spikelet, with spreading glumes to show the awned lemma with a short tuft of hair at the base, and (b) inner side of lemma with a hairy rachilla extending from the base. (4 × natural size.)

rhizomes; culms 30–100 cm long in compact tufts. The leaves are long, narrow and smooth, downy on the upper surface and smooth beneath; the ligule is quite short 1–3 mm long. The panicle is long, narrow, pale green or purplish with erect branches which close up after flowering. The spikelet is single-flowered. The lemma has a tuft of hairs at the base and a fine straight awn which barely protrudes from the spikelet. Flowering period: July to August.

Narrow Small-Reed is rare in the British Isles, growing in bogs and marshes. It is a variable species and identification may be further confused by the presence of hybrids between Narrow Small-Reed and Purple Small-Reed (16).

18 Yorkshire Fog
Holcus lanatus

A greyish-green perennial with compact tufts; culms 20–100 cm long. The leaves are soft and limp; the ligules are well-developed. The panicle is thick and downy, appearing reddish from one side and whitish from the other. It is open both during and after flowering. The compressed spikelet has two florets, the lower hermaphrodite, the upper male, the whole spikelet being shed at maturity. The glumes are longer than the lemmas and paleas. The lemma of the lower floret is awnless, that of the upper floret is equipped with a recurved awn which is hidden within the

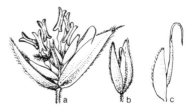

Yorkshire Fog (18) – (a) flowering spikelet with two florets, the lower bisexual, the upper male, (b) flowering spikelet containing a near mature seed. A ripe seed (c) surrounded by the persistent palea. The male flower continues to be attached to the seed. (4 × natural size.)

spikelet. Flowering period: May to August.

Yorkshire Fog grows in damp meadows and on drier soils such as roadsides, woods and fields. The grass may be considered as a weed in pastures and only has value as a fodder grass in poor, damp soils. The species is common throughout the British Isles, and Europe. Through cultivation it has been introduced into most areas with a temperate climate in both the Northern and Southern Hemispheres.

19 Creeping Soft-Grass
Holcus mollis

Perennial grass with horizontal, creeping rhizomes; culms 20–100 cm long, smooth apart from the nodes which bear a wreath of hairs. The blades are lightly hairy as are the lower sheaths;

the ligule is finely serrated. The whitish or purplish panicle is only open during flowering and closes up afterwards. The spikelet has an hermaphrodite floret and one male floret. The glumes are pointed. The awn of the male floret is bent and protrudes from the spikelet. Flowering period: June to August.

Creeping Soft-Grass grows on poor, acid and sandy soils, in scrub and woodland, where it carpets the ground with delicate, mainly sterile shoots. It can also appear as a weed in sandy soils and in some poor soils can be troublesome. The species is common throughout the British Isles and is widespread in Europe. Through cultivation it has been introduced into other areas of the world.

20 Grey Hair-Grass
Corynephorus canescens

A perennial which grows in close purplish blue-grey tufts; culms numerous, 10–35 cm long. The leaves are stiff, bristle-shaped and inrolled. The small pale reddish-mauve panicle has spreading branches during flowering, but is otherwise closed. The spikelet has two hermaphrodite florets. The

Creeping Soft-Grass (19) – (a) flowering spikelet, (b) spikelet after flowering, (c) the fertile female (lower) and male (upper floret with glumes removed, but each with the lemma in position. (3 × natural size.)

Grey Hair-Grass (20) – (a) spikelet, (b) two fertile florets surrounded by the lemma, but with glumes removed, (c) awn (a and b: 4 ×, c: 8 × natural size.)

membranous glumes are longer than the lemmas and paleas. The lemma is equipped with a very peculiar awn not found in our other grasses. The awn bears a ring of hairs dividing the upper, club-shaped part from the lower, twisted part which is hygroscopic. At maturity, the caryopsis falls invested in the lemma and palea. Flowering period: June to July.

Grey Hair-Grass only grows on poor, acid soil. A species of coastal sand-dunes, it may be locally very abundant. The roots tolerate drifting sand and subsequently help to bind it in place. The species is a rather rare grass in this country but is native to Norfolk, Suffolk, the Channel Isles and similar situations in Scandinavia, west and central Europe.

21 Early Hair-Grass
Aira praecox

An annual which grows in small tufts; culms 2–20 cm long. Leaves bristle-shaped, early withering. The oblong panicle is at first pale green and later golden brown. The short-stemmed spikelets are small and have two hermaphrodite florets. The glumes are membranous and longer than the lemmas and paleas. The lemma is finely bifid at the narrowed tip, and bears a slender awn which protrudes from the spikelet in varying degrees. Flowering period: April to June.

Early Hair-Grass is our

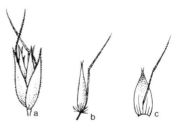

Early Hair-Grass (21) – (a) spikelet, (b) a floret surrounded by the lemma, (c) lemma as seen from the dorsal side. (5 × natural size.)

smallest species of grass. It grows on open, poor, acid or sandy soil where most other plants do not. The seeds germinate in the autumn and the growing period is during the damp autumn and winter months. The summer is unfavourable for this plant and when the soil dries out, the grass withers, the seeds remaining dormant until autumn.

The species is common on sandy and dry slopes throughout the British Isles, central and western Europe, being most common in coastal areas with mild winters.

22 Silvery Hair-Grass
Aira caryophyllea

A delicate annual; the culms 3–40 cm long, reddish. The leaves are bristle-shaped. The spreading panicle has thread-like branches and mauvish-silver spikelets. Flowering period: May to July.

Silvery Hair-Grass grows in similar places to the previous species and can also occur as a weed in poor, acid, sandy soils. It is common throughout the British Isles and Europe. It also grows in Africa's high mountains, South Africa and has been introduced into America and Australia.

HAIR-GRASS

The species of Hair-Grass, *Deschampsia* are all perennials. The spikelets each have two florets with membranous glumes which give the panicle its characteristic silvery tinge. The glumes are approximately the same length as the spikelet. The lemma has a fine wreath of hairs at the base and a membranous serrated tip; a thin, straight or bent awn extends from the base. There are about sixty species of which four may be found in the British Isles.

23 Tufted Hair-Grass
Deschampsia caespitosa

A large, densely tufted perennial with many sterile leafy shoots and withered sheaths; culms up to 1 metre long. The long flat leaf-blades are quite rough at the edges and on the ribs; the deep grooves between the ribs can be seen as lighter

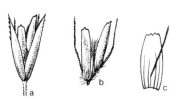

*Tufted Hair-Grass (23) – (a) spikelet,
(b) two florets surrounded by lemmas,
but with the glumes removed. The axis
of the spikelet is hairy, and continues as
the rachilla above the florets. The lemma
(c) as seen from dorsal side. (4 ×
natural size.)*

stripes. The panicle is pyramid-
shaped with horizontal
branches. The spikelets are pale
brownish or mauve with a
silvery tinge. The glumes are
membranous. The lemma has
a short, straight awn which
barely protrudes from the spikelet. Flowering period: June to
August.

Tufted Hair-Grass grows on
wet, poorly drained soils. When
young, the grass is sometimes
eaten by animals but is generally worthless as a fodder crop.
It is common throughout the
British Isles, often abundant in
marshy fields, rough grassland
and moorland. It is widely
distributed in the Arctic and
temperate regions and in mountainous districts of tropical
Africa, South America and
Australia.

24 Wavy Hair-Grass
Deschampsia flexuosa

A loose, dark green, tufted
perennial with numerous sterile
shoots; culms 20–100 cm long.
The leaves are soft and thread-
like; the ligule is short and
rounded. The medium-sized,
spreading panicle remains open
after flowering and has fine
wavy branches. The spikelet
is reddish-brown and silver
tinged. The glumes are membranous and transparent. The
lemma has a delicate, bent awn
which protrudes from the spikelet. Flowering period: June to
July.

Wavy Hair-Grass is associ-
ated with poor, acid conditions
and grows on heaths and sandy
soils. It tolerates shade and will
grow in pine woods but seldom
flowers there. However, it
flowers abundantly in clearings
in woods and heaths which have
been cleared or ploughed
recently. From a distance it is
easily recognised by the fine,
delicate reddish-brown
panicles.

The species is common
throughout the British Isles and
widespread throughout the
world in the temperate zones of
the Northern Hemisphere, in
mountainous districts of the
Tropics and in Patagonia.

25 Yellow or Golden Oat-Grass
Trisetum flavescens

A loose, tuft-forming perennial; the culms yellowish-green, 20–80 cm long. The leaf-sheaths and blades are hairy; the ligule is very short and the margin serrated. The shining, golden panicle has wide open branches during flowering, otherwise it is tightly closed. The spikelets are 5–7 mm long, compressed, with two to four, but usually three florets. The glumes are keeled and slightly shorter than the spikelet. The lemma is membranous with a bifid tip and a bent awn which protrudes from the spikelet. Flowering period: June to July.

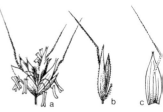

Yellow or Golden Oat-Grass (25) – (a) a flowering spikelet with three florets (b) the uppermost floret surrounded by the lemma and palea. The axis of the spikelet continues above the florets as a hairy rachilla. The lemma (c) of the flower spread out and seen from the dorsal side (3 × natural size.)

Golden Oat-Grass is found on road verges and in old pastures. It is not a native and probably came from the central European mountain districts, where it is a valuable fodder grass. It was formerly used in seed mixtures for pasture and hay and is well-liked by cattle and sheep. The species is now widespread throughout the world growing wild after cultivation.

OATS

The Aveneae tribe of the Gramineae is a group of perennial and annual grasses with large, two- to many-flowered spikelets, convex glumes which are usually as long as, or longer than the rest of the spikelet and a lemma which is bifid at the tip and provided with a bent awn which extends from the back; the awn is twisted below the middle and is capable of making hygroscopic movements, i.e. in damp conditions it straightens out and bends and twists itself back into shape when dry.

The Aveneae consists of several genera and the botanical name *Avena* has been reserved for a group of annual species which includes our cultivated Oats. These species will be discussed in more detail with the cereals (85). The perennial species belong to two different genera: *Arrhenatherum* and *Avenula*. Species of *Arrhenatherum* have two-flowered spikelets with a male, awn-bearing floret below and an hermaphrodite floret above. There are six species, one of which is British.

Species of *Avenula* have many-flowered spikelets, and the florets are all hermaphrodite and awn bearing. There are about ninety species, of which two are British.

26 Tall Oat-Grass
Arrhenatherum elatius

Perennial with loose tufts; culms 50–150 cm long, smooth. The leaves are slightly rough, yellowish-green, shiny on both sides, the upper surface has low, flat ribs and the underside is keeled; the ligule is quite long. The panicle is narrow and up to 30 cm long, sometimes pale green; the branches are spreading during flowering, but later contracted. The spikelet is erect with two florets, the lower male, the upper hermaphrodite, falling together at maturity. The lemma of the male floret bears a long awn, that of the hermaphrodite floret is awnless. Flowering period: June to September.

Frequently used as a fodder grass and also for the seeding of road verges and railway embankments. The species is found in hedgerows on rough grassland, roadsides and waste ground. It occurs in Britain, Europe, northern Africa, western Asia, but with cultivation has also spread to temperate zones throughout the world.

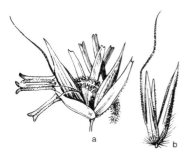

Tall Oat-Grass (26) – (a) flowering spikelet. The lower floret of the spikelet is a male and bears an awn-bearing lemma while the upper floret is bisexual and is awnless. The two florets (b) with glumes removed. (3 × natural size.)

27 Meadow Oat-Grass
Avenula pratensis

A densely tufted, blue-green perennial; culms 30–80 cm long. The leaves are stiff and rough. The silvery panicle is narrow with short branches, each bearing one or two spikelets. Spikelets are up to 3·5 cm long with three to six, but usually four, florets. Lemma equipped with a strong, bent awn. Flowering period: June to July.

Meadow Oat-Grass grows on dry, uncultivated, grassy banks and especially on chalk and limestone. It is widely distributed throughout the country and also throughout most of Europe, northern Africa and the Near East.

28 Hairy Oat-Grass
Avenula pubescens

Loose tufted perennial; culms 30–100 cm long. The leaves are green, sometimes purple, soft, the lower hairy, the upper often smooth. The panicle is green or purplish, each branch with one to three spikelets. The spikelets are about 1·5 cm long with two to four but usually three florets. The lemma bears a long, bent awn. Flowering period: May to July.

Hairy Oat-Grass grows on

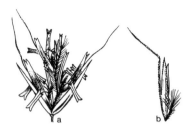

Hairy Oat-Grass (28) – (a) flowering spikelet. The axis of the spikelet is hairy and the tip ends in a very small barren floret. A single floret (b) surrounded by the lemma. The hairy rachilla can be seen at the base. (1½ × natural size.)

commons, meadows, uncultivated banks, hill slopes and roadside verges. It is widespread in Europe and western Asia.

29 Common Reed-Grass
Phragmites australis

A perennial with stolons and thick creeping branched rhizomes; the erect culms are 1·5–3 metres long. The leaf-blades are 20–60 cm long and 1–3 cm wide, the margin rough; the ligule is a fringe of hairs. The panicle is dark purple, large and many flowered. The spikelet is 10–16 mm long with two to six florets, the lowermost male, the others hermaphrodite; the axis of the spikelet is covered with long, silky hairs. The glumes are shorter than the spikelet. The lemma has no awn. Flowering period: August to October.

Common Reed-Grass, which is often called 'reed' or, incorrectly 'rush' is the largest species to be found in the British Isles. It grows in close stands in fresh or brackish water and at the edges of rivers and lakes to form 'reed swamps', which often extend over large areas. It is sometimes found in damp meadows but suffers from heavy grazing. In winter, the Common Reed loses its leaves and the culms die down. The stiff, withered straws remain standing throughout the winter. In the following spring, growth is slow and the plants do not reach their full height until summer. It has some use to man since the dried straws are used for thatching, as a base for plastering, and for the making of mats. The straws are harvested in the autumn or winter when the ground is hardened by frost. It is common throughout the British Isles and is widespread throughout the temperate regions of the world.

30 Purple Moor-Grass
Molinia caerulea

A compact, densely tufted perennial; culms 15–120 cm long, with only one node towards the base. The leaves have long, narrow, slightly hairy blades; the ligule is a fringe of hairs. The panicle is dark bluish or purple, with thin branches that are open during flowering, but are otherwise contracted. The spikelets are small, somewhat elongate and usually three-flowered. The glumes are shorter than the spikelet. The lemmas are awnless. The anthers and styles are dark purple. Flowering period: July to September.

Purple Moor-Grass grows in damp peaty areas and is found mainly in poor, acid marshes, on damp moorlands, heaths and commons. It can often form large stands and dominate the

Common Reed-Grass (29) – (a) *flowering spikelet*, (b) *a single floret, surrounded by the lemma and palea. Note the hairy rachilla.* (a 2 × *and* b 3 × *natural size.*)

Purple Moor-Grass (30) – (a) hairy ligule, (b) a flowering spikelet. (2 × natural size.)

local vegetation. The leaves and culms die down in the winter and only the lowest node of the culm remains green and swollen, containing food reserves for the new shoots which will develop in the following spring. The lowest node can remain in position for many years as a stiff, pointed process even when the nutrient has expired, making the tuft firm and prickly. The grass has no particular value as fodder but was previously used as a bedding material for animals. Purple Moor-Grass is common throughout the British Isles, Europe, northern Africa and western and northern Asia.

31 Heath Grass
Sieglingia decumbens

A densely tufted perennial; culms 10–60 cm long, often prostrate at the base, then growing erect from a node. The flat, somewhat stiff leaves are greyish-green and slightly hairy on the upper surface, but shiny green below; the ligule is a dense fringe of short hairs. The panicle is slender with erect branches. The glistening spikelets have four to six florets. The glumes are about the same length as the spikelet. The lemma is hairy at the base and three-toothed at the tip, becoming tough and leathery. Flowering period: June to August.

The flowers of Heath Grass are cleistogamous, i.e. self-pollination takes place within the closed florets. However, normal flowering has been observed in this species, especially in wet conditions. It often produces spikelets at the base of the old culms; these are pale with one or two florets and produce

Heath Grass (31) – (a) spikelet, (b) the lemma from the dorsal side, note the three-toothed tip, (c) a seed enveloped in the leathery lemma. (a 2 × natural size, b and c 3 × natural size.)

viable seed. Heath Grass grows on poor, acid, often somewhat damp soil on moors, grassland in woods, paths and roadsides. The species is common throughout the British Isles, Europe, northern Africa and south-west Asia in mountain areas. It is thought to have originated in eastern Canada.

32 Somerset Grass
Koeleria valesiana

A densely tufted bluish-grey perennial; culms 10–40 cm long, surrounded at the base by withered sheaths. Leaves stiff, narrow and inrolled; ligules very short. The inflorescence is a narrow spike-like panicle. The compressed wedge-shaped spikelets are glistening and silvery with two to three florets. The glumes are pointed. The lemma is awnless. Flowering period: June to August.

Somerset Grass is a rare plant, found on limestone hills in Somerset. It occurs in western

Europe and northern Africa. It is easily distinguished from the common Crested Hair-Grass by the dense layers of withered reticulate sheaths at the base of the culms.

33 Crested Hair-Grass
Koeleria macrantha

A tufted perennial; culms 10–60 cm long. Leaves bright green. The panicle is lobed. The silvery spikelets have two to four florets. The lemmas are pointed. Flowering period: June to July.

Crested Hair-Grass grows on dry grasslands and chalk hills and is common in the British Isles. The species is widespread in Europe, Asia and North America.

34 Crested Dogs-Tail
Cynosurus cristatus

Small, densely tufted perennial; culms 5–75 cm long. The leaves are narrow, often folded lengthwise; the ligules short. The panicle is green, narrow and one-sided, with a wavy axis; each node of the axis bears two spikelets, one of which is fertile, and the other sterile; the fertile spikelet contains two to five hermaphrodite florets and is partially covered by the sterile

Crested Hair-Grass (33) – (a) *a two-flowered spikelet,* (b) *the same for Somerset Grass (32). (2 × natural size.)* size.)

Crested Dogs Tail (34) – (a) a portion of the raceme with dense flowering spikelets, (b) a three-flowered spikelet. (a 2 × and b 4 × natural size.)

one. The lemmas of the fertile florets have short awns. Flowering period: June to August.

Crested Dogs-Tail grows in meadows, on commons and roadside verges. It has been used in the past to seed permanent grass paths and lawns in this country, although it is used infrequently nowadays. It becomes very noticeable towards the autumn as the tough culms are not grazed by animals. The species is common throughout the British Isles, Europe, south-west Asia and through cultivation, other temperate regions of the Northern and Southern Hemispheres.

35 Blue Moor-Grass
Sesleria calcaria

A dense, flat, tufted perennial; culms 10–45 cm long. The leaves are short, narrow, somewhat folded lengthwise, with plicate tips, bluish-grey above, dark green underneath; the ligule is quite short. The panicle is spike-like and blue-violet, and invested at the base with short, broad scales. The two-flowered spikelets have very short stalks. The glumes are pointed and nearly as long as the spikelet. The lemma has prominent nerves which extend into pointed apical teeth. Flowering period: April to June.

Blue Moor-Grass is a species of pastures and hill grassland, frequently on limestone. It is common in northern England, western Ireland and parts of Scotland. It also occurs in central and southern Europe and Iceland.

36 Cocksfoot
Dactylis glomerata

A somewhat grey-green, strongly tufted perennial; culms few, 15–140 cm long, stiff, smooth. The leaf shoots are compressed with tough edges; the somewhat rough blades are long and broad, with strong keels; the ligule is long. The panicle is large, consisting of a dense one-sided mass of green spikelets. The spikelets are compressed and contain two to five florets. The glumes are invested with stiff hairs. The lemma is hairy along the keel and it gradually tapers to a pointed tip. Flowering period: June to September.

Cocksfoot is an important cultivated grass which is grown in large quantities for hay and pastures. The young shoots remain green throughout the winter protected by the withering older sheaths and the grass grows again quickly in the spring. It must be cut before the culms develop as they are too coarse for fodder. In permanent grass paths Cocksfoot is inclined to form large, untidy tufts, which die from the middle. The grass is sometimes sown in mixtures on roadside banks and railway embankments. It is a very common grass and is found throughout the British Isles on roadsides and banks. Cocksfoot probably originated in Europe, North Africa and Asia, but due to cultivation is now widespread in all temperate regions of the world.

A similar species, Wood Cocksfoot (*Dactylis polygama*) has become naturalised in Buckinghamshire woodlands.

37 Common Quaking Grass
Briza media

A loosely tufted perennial; culms 15–75 cm long. The leaves are bluish-green, narrow, and rather rough. The panicle is large and spreading with wavy, hair-fine branches. The nodding spikelets are comparatively large, heart-shaped, with four to twelve florets. The glumes are convex and finely pointed. The slightest breeze sets the spikelets in motion, hence the name, Quaking Grass. Flowering period: June to August.

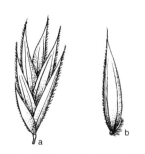

Cocksfoot (36) – (a) spikelet, (b) a ripening seed surrounded by the lemma and palea, and the rachilla. (4 × natural size.)

Common Quaking-Grass (37) – (a) spikelet, (b) the lemma, (c) the dorsal side of the lemma. (4 × natural size.)

Common Quaking Grass is one of our most beautiful and easily recognised wild species of grass. It grows in meadows and occasionally on dry grassy banks, especially on chalky soils. It is common throughout the British Isles and over most of Europe.

MELICK

The species of Melick, *Melica*, are perennials with closed, tubular sheaths. The slightly compressed, four-flowered spikelets are often beautifully coloured. The glumes are nearly as long as the spikelet, convex and membranous with three to five nerves. The spikelet has two to three sterile lemmas which form a club-shaped body above the fertile florets. The awnless fertile lemmas have seven to nine nerves.

38 Wood Melick
Melica uniflora

Perennial with slender, creeping rhizomes; culms 20–60 cm long, erect. The leaves are thin, fresh-green; sheaths tubular, the upper ones having a bristle 1–4 mm long at the mouth of the sheath opposite to the blade; ligules short. The panicle is open with long, upright and spreading branches which bear one to six spikelets. Each spikelet has one fertile floret and two or three sterile lemmas. The fertile lemmas and paleas are green. The glumes are convex, reddish-brown. Flowering period: May to June.

Wood Melick is common throughout the British Isles except in northern Scotland, in woods with humus rich soil. It usually forms a close uniform carpet in older open beech-woods. The species is also widespread in Europe and can be found in south-west Asia.

39 Mountain or Nodding Melick
Melica nutans

Is similar to 38 but is easily distinguished by the narrow, one-sided panicle, and the nodding spikelets which for the most part are placed singly on short branches. The spikelets have two to three fertile florets and

Wood Melick (38) – (a) flowering spikelet, (b) a ripe seed of the same surrounded by the lemma and palea and with an attached sterile floret. Flowering spikelet (c) of Nodding Melick (39). Flowering spikelet (d) of Hairy Melick (40). Ligule (e) of Wood Melick (38). (a, c and d 2 ×, and b and e 3 × natural size.)

one to two sterile lemmas at the tip, the florets falling together when ripe. The glumes are reddish-brown with wide white membranous margins. Flowering period: May to July.

Nodding Melick is found in rich soil, but does not tolerate as much shade as Wood Melick and is therefore found more on wood margins, spinneys and similar places. The species is fairly rare in this country, although widespread in mountains of Europe, northern and south-west Asia.

40   Hairy Melick
Melica ciliata

A tuft-forming perennial with short rhizomes; culms stiff, erect, 20–60 cm long. Leaves narrow, quite stiff and greyish-green. Panicle spike-like, whitish or purplish. The spikelets contain one fertile floret in

addition to the sterile lemmas. The glumes are pointed. The lemma of the fertile floret is covered with long silky hairs, which during flowering, protrude from the spikelet giving the whole panicle a strikingly hairy appearance. Flowering period: May to June.

Hairy Melick is found in most of Europe, North Africa and the Near East, but is only cultivated for ornamental purposes in this country.

41   Water Whorl-Grass
Catabrosa aquatica

A perennial with creeping stolons which root at the nodes; culms 5–75 cm long, erect. The leaves have compressed sheaths and fairly short, broad blades with blunt tips. The violet-tinged panicle is much branched. The spikelet has one to three florets. The glumes are

97

Spikelets of (a) *Water Whorl-Grass (41);* (b) *and* (c) *Love Grass (42),* (b) *with unripe and* (c) *with ripe seeds. In* (c) *the majority of the flowers have dropped the seeds and lower glumes already and only the palea of the flower remains on the axis of the spikelet. A seed and the lower glume are shown in* (d). *(4 × natural size.)*

much shorter than the spikelet. The lemmas are awnless. Flowering period: May to July.

Water Whorl-Grass grows in muddy margins of ponds, slow-running streams, ditches and swampy places, especially on rich soils. The grass is very palatable to animals, but cannot easily be cultivated as fodder due to its special growth requirements. It is widespread, but rather local throughout the country, and recently has diminished, probably due to land drainage. It is widespread in the temperate regions of the Northern Hemisphere.

42 Love Grass
Eragrostis minor

An annual; the stems 5–30 cm long, branching at the base and somewhat geniculate. The leaves are hairy; the ligule is a tuft of long hairs. The violet-tinged panicle is large and open, with spreading branches. The spikelets are compressed, with five to twenty florets. Glumes ovate, considerably shorter than the spikelet. The lemma is ovate with three prominent nerves, falling with the seed at maturity; the palea is persistent. Flowering period: July to October.

A grass of the Mediterranean and south-east Europe, Love Grass is grown as an ornamental in Britain.

MEADOW-GRASS

The species of Meadow-Grass, *Poa*, have keeled leaf-sheaths, folded leaf-blades when young; the tips are hooded. The panicles have compressed two- to ten-flowered spikelets. The glumes are shorter than the spikelet and both the glumes and lemmas are keeled. The five-nerved lemma has a thin and membranous tip and a tuft of cottony hairs at the base. Awns, when present are very short. At maturity, the rhachilla breaks beneath each floret, the caryopsis remaining enclosed in the lemma and palea.

There are some 300 species of Meadow-Grass, fifteen of which are British. Many are important fodder grasses.

43 Annual Meadow-Grass
Poa annua

Annual or short-lived perennial, in small, compact knotted tufts; culms 3–30 cm long. The thin leaves are often wrinkled; the sheaths are compressed; the ligule is up to 5 mm long, shorter on the lower leaves. The branches of the spreading panicle droop after flowering. The spikelets are ovate, 3–10 mm long, with three to ten florets. The glumes are considerably shorter than the spikelet, the lower small with only one nerve, the upper with three nerves.

Annual Meadow-Grass produces seed throughout the year, quickly appearing on soil kept open and free from other vegetation, e.g. on cultivated ground, garden paths, yards, between flagstones, on pavements, on woodland paths and roadsides, etc. Short-lived perennial varieties with rooting stolons may occur in shady places.

The species is found through-out the British Isles and is widespread throughout the world.

44 Smooth Meadow-Grass
Poa pratensis

A perennial, greyish-green or pale bluish-green grass with creeping rhizomes; culms 10–40 cm long, smooth. The tips of the leaves may be blunt or pointed; the ligules are short, 1–3 mm and truncate. The panicle is compact before flowering, later spreading and pyramid-shaped, green or violet-tinged. The spikelets are 4–6 mm long with two to five florets. The glumes are much the same size; the upper with three nerves, the lower with one (rarely three). Flowering period: May to July.

Several strains of Smooth Meadow-Grass occur in Britain, some of which are apomictic, i.e. capable of setting seed without fertilisation. It is widespread throughout the British Isles, especially in meadows and pastures and on roadsides. It

Ligules of (a) *Smooth Meadow-Grass* (*44*) *and* (b) *Rough Meadow-Grass* (*45*). (*3 × natural size.*)

grows on a variety of soils but prefers well-drained situations. An important fodder grass on the Continent and in North America, its main use in Britain is for sowing banks, roadsides and, in mixtures, for sports-fields.

45 Rough Meadow-Grass
Poa trivialis

A perennial with creeping, leafy stolons forming loose tufts; culms 20 – 100 cm long. The sheaths are rough; the ligules up to 10 mm long. The panicle is large and spreading. The spike-lets are two- to four-flowered. Flowering period: June to July.

Rough Meadow-Grass grows on damp, rich soil and in Britain is commonly found in meadows, along ditches and in damp woodlands. It is an excellent fodder grass. It probably origin-ated in Europe and temperate parts of Asia, but due to cultiva-tion is now widely distributed throughout the world.

46 Wood Meadow-Grass
Poa nemoralis

A loosely tufted perennial; culms thin 15–90 cm long, with brown nodes. The leaves are green and hairless; the ligules very short. The panicle is some-what nodding with fine branches, which during flower-ing are spreading and later erect. The one- to five-flowered spikelets are 3–6 mm long. Flowering period: June to July.

Wood Meadow-Grass grows in deciduous woods, commons and parks and is found in most parts of the British Isles. It is widespread throughout the temperate regions of the Northern Hemisphere, and has spread to South America and New Zealand.

47 Swamp Meadow-Grass
Poa palustris

Densely tufted perennial; culms 30–150 cm long, smooth, cylin-drical. The leaf-sheaths are smooth, the lower slightly keeled; the ligule is long. The brownish panicle is large, and spreading. The two- to five-flowered spikelets are 3–5 mm long. The lemma has faint nerves and a brownish membranous margin. Flowering period: June to July.

Swamp Meadow-Grass grows in damp meadows, at the edges of ponds and in fens. The species is comparatively rare, occurring mainly in the lowlands. It was introduced in the 19th Century as a fodder grass in irrigated fields. Since then it has become widespread in this country. It is also widespread in the temperate regions of the Northern Hemisphere.

Swamp Meadow-Grass can be distinguished from large, robust plants of Wood Meadow-Grass by its long ligules and leaf-sheaths and from Rough Meadow-Grass by the smooth leaf-sheaths. It can be distinguished from Smooth Meadow-Grass by its longer ligules and the absence of rhizomes.

48 Flattened Meadow-Grass
Poa compressa

A slender perennial with wiry rhizomes; culms 10–60 cm long, flattened, tough, greyish-green. The sheaths are strongly compressed; the ligule is short. The bluish-green or yellowish panicle is contracted. The spikelets are 3–8 mm long with three to ten florets. Flowering period: June to August.

Flattened Meadow-Grass grows on banks, roadsides, and on waste ground, commonly on shallow, well-drained soil. Though of no value as a fodder crop it is quite common in the British Isles apart from northern Scotland, Ireland and Wales. It is also widespread in Europe, and has through cultivation, spread throughout North and South America, eastern Asia and Australia.

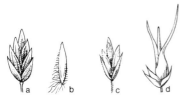

Smooth Meadow-Grass (44) – (a) spikelet, (b) ripe seed surrounded by lemma. Spikelet (c) of Wood Meadow-Grass (46). Viviparous spikelet (d) of Bulbous Meadow-Grass (49). (3 × natural size.)

49 Bulbous Meadow-Grass
Poa bulbosa

A slender tufted perennial; culms 5–40 cm long. The

sheaths are swollen and bulbous at the base; the leaves are greyish-green, stiff and narrow; the ligule is short and white-membranous. The panicle is small and dense with three- to six-flowered spikelets. Flowering period: March to May.

The grass soon withers and dies down, leaving the bulbous bases. These contain food reserves and can sprout when conditions are favourable. The bases may become detached and dispersed by the wind, each giving rise to a new plant. One variety of Bulbous Meadow-Grass has the upper part of the spikelet replaced by a bulbil. This may produce roots and also give rise to a new plant.

Bulbous Meadow-Grass is a rare species of open sandy and grassy areas, in southern and eastern Britain. It is widespread in the Mediterranean countries and western Europe.

SALT-MARSH-GRASS

The Salt-Marsh-Grasses, *Puccinellia*, have cylindrical, several-flowered spikelets, glumes shorter than the spikelet and a convex lemma with five distinct nerves and a membranous broadly rounded tip. There are 100 species of which five are British.

50 Common Salt-Marsh-Grass
Puccinellia maritima

A bluish-green densely tufted perennial with creeping rooting stolons; culms 10–80 cm long, stiff, erect. The leaves are smooth, folded in the lower part and with a slender, hooded tip; the ligule is short. The panicle is rather stiff. The cylindrical three- to ten-flowered spikelets are violet-tinged. Flowering period: June to July.

Common Salt-Marsh-Grass is an important plant of salt marshes but may also occur on sand, shingle and inland brackish areas. Where the plant colonises bare coastal mud it forms a continuous turf. With each immersion by the tide, the foliage filters out the silt and debris, helping to raise the level of the marsh. The species is distributed around the shores of the British Isles and is widespread along Europe's coasts from north Norway to the Mediterranean, and along the

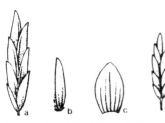

Common Salt-Marsh-Grass (50) – (a) spikelet, (b) a ripening seed of the same species, surrounded by the lemma, (c) dorsal surface of lower glume of the same. Spikelet (d) of Reflexed Salt-Marsh-Grass (51). (3 × natural size.)

North American east coast.

It may be distinguished from the other species of Salt-Marsh-Grass by the stolons and the longer spikelets and lemmas.

51 Reflexed Salt-Marsh-Grass
Puccinellia distans

A perennial, very rarely annual, which forms dense tufts; culms 10–60 cm long, bent at the base. The greyish-green leaves are narrow and flat or rolled; the ligule is short. The panicle is large and open during and after flowering, the branches bare for half their length, becoming deflexed. The spikelets have three to nine florets. Flowering period: June to July.

Reflexed Salt-Marsh-Grass grows on the higher ground of salt marshes and may also be found inland on damp soil with a large concentration of salt, e.g. dunghills, rubbish tips and at the edges of village ponds, etc. It is common along the shores of the British Isles except northern Scotland and Northern Ireland and is also widespread throughout the Northern Hemisphere.

SWEET GRASS

The Sweet Grass genus, *Glyceria*, comprises perennials with leaves folded along the mid-rib and sheaths which are tubular almost up to the blade. The panicles have cylindrical spikelets, each with several florets. The glumes are considerably shorter than the whole spikelet. The lemma is convex and has seven to nine strong nerves which do not anastamose at the tip. There is no awn. There are forty species, four British.

The name is a reference to the sweetness of the seeds, and of the young stems.

52 Reed Sweet-Grass
Glyceria maxima

A perennial with horizontal rhizomes; culms erect, 1–2·5 metres long. The sheaths are compressed, keeled, entire when young, later splitting. The leaves are long, broad and strongly keeled; the ligule is 3–6 mm long. The richly branched panicle is 15–45 cm long, with erect, spreading branches, pale green at first, later becoming brownish-purple. The ovate spikelets have four to ten florets. Flowering period: June to August.

Reed Sweet-Grass grows on rich mud along streams and lakes, in deeper water than other species and sometimes forming extensive pure stands. Animals like to eat the young culms, but these later become coarse and unpalatable. The species is common throughout the British Isles and is also widespread in Europe and northern Asia.

53 Floating Sweet-Grass
Glyceria fluitans

A loosely tufted perennial with long creeping and rooting, or floating stolons; culms 40–100 cm long, prostrate at the base

Spikelet (a) *of Floating Sweet-Grass* (*53*). *Spikelet* (b) *of Reed Sweet-Grass* (*52*). *Lemma* (c) *of Floating Sweet-Grass.* (a *and* b 1½ ×, c 2 × *natural size.*)

and then ascending. The sheaths are compressed and the margins fused; the ligule is long and pointed. The panicle is long and narrow, the branches usually in pairs, sometimes solitary, spreading during flowering, otherwise appressed to the axis of the panicle. The spikelet is eight- to sixteen-flowered, cylindrical and up to 3·5 cm long. The lemma is pointed. Flowering period: June to July.

Floating Sweet-Grass grows in abundance in and by fresh water, at pond edges, ditches and in marshes. The succulent foliage is a favourite of cattle. The species is common throughout the British Isles and also widespread in Europe, northern

Africa and the Near East and introduced into North America and Australia.

Another common species, Plicate Sweet-Grass, *Glyceria plicata* can be distinguished from Floating Sweet-Grass by the shorter lemmas and smaller anthers. Hybrids between these two species are widespread in Britain.

FESCUE

The Fescue genus, *Festuca*, comprises many perennial grasses, with many-flowered spikelets. The glumes are shorter than the lemma of the closest floret. The lemma is convex at the back and the nerves anastamose at the tip. The tips of the lemma and palea sometimes bear awns or beards. The ripe caryopsis is invested in the lemma and palea, the floret falls entire at maturity. There are about eighty species, eleven of which are British.

54 Giant Fescue
Festuca gigantea

A loosely tufted perennial; culms 45–150 cm long, smooth with brown nodes. The leaves are up to 16 mm wide, limp, shining dark green below, dull greyish-green above. The top of the sheath has two prominent spreading auricles at the apex; the lower sheaths are often deep purple; the ligule is short. The panicle is up to 50 cm long with long, thin spreading or drooping branches. The spikelets are three- to ten-flowered. The lemmas and paleas have long, rough, wavy awns. Flowering period: July to August.

Giant Fescue grows in deciduous woods and shady places with damp peaty soil, especially where the nitrogen content is high. It is common throughout

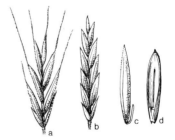

Spikelet (a) *of Giant Fescue* (54). *Spikelet* (b) *of Meadow Fescue* (55) *and its seed viewed from* (c) *its lateral and* (d) *its dorsal sides.* (a *and* b 1½ ×, c *and* d 3 × *natural size.*)

the British Isles and is wide-spread throughout Europe and northern Asia.

55 Meadow Fescue
Festuca pratensis

A perennial forming loose tufts; culms 30–120 cm long. The leaves are rather broad, flat and sometimes rough; the sheaths have narrow spreading auricles at the apex, the ligules are very short. The rather one-sided erect or somewhat nodding panicle has branches in pairs, spreading during flowering; otherwise contracted. The spikelets are 10–20 mm long with five to fourteen greenish, or more seldom violet-tinged florets. The lemmas are awnless. Flowering period: June to August.

Meadow Fescue is an important fodder grass in the British Isles. It is mixed with other grasses or clover for short-term or permanent grass fields and is suitable for both hay and grazing. It is also used in grass seed mixtures for verges. The species is spread over Europe and northern Asia and through cultivation has spread to other temperate regions of the Northern and Southern Hemispheres.

56 Tall Fescue
Festuca arundinacea

A robust perennial in large, rough tufts; culms 45–200 cm long. The leaf-sheaths bear narrow, spreading, minutely hairy auricles at the apex. The panicle is erect or nodding, spreading or contracted, the unequal branches usually in pairs. The spikelets are three- to tenflowered. The lemma has no awn, or only a very short one. Flowering period: June to August.

The various varieties of Tall Fescue grow in very distinct habitats. The taller varieties are found on heavy soils and by river margins. The smaller, less robust varieties occur on drier lighter soils in pastures and on grazed land. The Tall Fescue found in Britain is too tough and stiff to be used as fodder, though some varieties have been used as pasture grasses. It is found in Europe and northern Asia, but has become very widespread through cultivation.

It may be distinguished from Meadow Fescue by the minutely hairy auricles and by having three or more spikelets on the shorter of each pair of panicle branches.

57 Sheep's Fescue
Festuca ovina

A small, densely tufted perennial; culms 50–70 cm long. The leaves are less than 0·6 mm wide, threadlike, soft. The panicle is small with erect branches. The spikelets are 5–10 mm long, violet-tinged, three-to nine-flowered. The lemma has a short awn. Flowering period: May to July.

Sheep's Fescue is a characteristic plant of dry, poor soil and is common throughout the British Isles on heaths, moors, dry fields and hills. Despite its lack of foliage, the grass is nutritious and is valuable as a fodder crop in poor areas. There are many varieties of this species, which are widespread in the temperate regions of the Northern Hemisphere and through cultivation in the Southern Hemisphere.

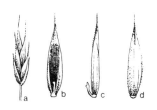

Sheep's Fescue (57) – (a) *spikelet*, (b)–(d) *seed viewed respectively from the ventral, lateral and dorsal surfaces.* (a 2 ×, b–d 4 × natural size.)

58 Red or Creeping Fescue
Festuca rubra ssp. *rubra*

A perennial with slender, creeping rhizomes; culms 15–90 cm long. The leaves are long, soft, bristle-shaped, the lower in-rolled, the upper usually flat. The reddish sheaths have small rounded auricles; the ligule is very short. The three- to nine-flowered spikelets are usually reddish-purple. The lemmas have short awns at the tips. Flowering period: May to July.

Red Fescue is widely distributed in the British Isles, growing in most conditions except deep shade. It is often the most abundant species of meadows and on good soil produces excellent grazing, though little hay. The species includes a large number of varieties and is widespread throughout the Northern Hemisphere.

59 Squirrel-Tail Fescue
Vulpia bromoides

A loosely tufted annual; culms 5–60 cm long. Leaves narrow. The panicle is erect and one-sided with short contracted branches which are slightly swollen at the tips. The spikelets have five to ten florets. The glumes are short; the lemmas long awned. Stamen usually solitary, often remaining enclosed between the lemma and palea at the top of the mature caryopsis. Flowering period: May to July.

Squirrel-Tail Fescue grows on dry slopes, chalk hills and on poor, sandy heaths, often forming large masses on open ground. Frequent in the British Isles, the species is also widespread in the Mediterranean countries, western Europe, mountain districts of tropical Africa and has been introduced throughout the Northern and Southern Hemispheres through cultivation.

The name 'squirrel tail' is analogous to the names 'fox tail' and 'cat's tail', referring to the roughly hairy panicle.

BROME

The species of Brome, *Bromus* may be annual, biennial or perennial. The margins of the sheath are fused to form a tube. The ligule is membranous and often ragged. The inflorescence is a panicle with long branches. The spikelets are one- to many-flowered. The glumes are unequal and considerably shorter than the spikelet. The lemmas have nerves coming to a point at the tip and may be awnless or with a short awn. The two stigmas are borne on the side of a hairy, lobed appendage situated on top of the ovary. This appendage persists on the ripe caryopsis and is a diagnostic feature of *Bromus*.

The spikelets look very different in the many species of Brome but fall into three groups, which are sometimes considered as separate genera:

Section I: *Anisantha* is identified by the spikelets being wedge shaped and broadest towards the tip after flowering. The glumes are very short, the lower one having only one nerve, the upper three. The lemma is compressed with a sharply defined keel and has a long awn which is just as long as, or longer than the lemma itself. There are about fifteen annual or biennial species, four of which are found in the British Isles.

Section II: *Zerna* has oblong, compressed spikelets which do not spread out at the top. The glumes are short and are similarly one and three nerved. The lemma is compressed and keeled and the awn is comparatively short or absent. There are about twenty-five perennial species, four occurring in the British Isles.

Section III: *Bromus* in the strict sense, comprises species with oval or cylindrical spikelets, glumes with respectively three to five, and five to seven nerves and convex lemmas without a keel; the awn is comparatively short. There are about fifty perennial species, seven of which are found in the British Isles.

60 Drooping Brome
Bromus tectorum

Annual; culms 10–60 cm long, softly hairy and branched from the base. The leaves are hairy; the ligule is short. The panicle is one-sided, often purplish with spreading branches. The nodding four- to eight-flowered spikelets are compressed, becoming wedge shaped. The glumes are sharply keeled. The awn of the lemma is as long as, or longer than the lemma. The caryopsis is hairy at the tip and tightly enclosed by the lemma and palea. Flowering period: May to July.

A Mediterranean species, naturalised (but rare) in Norfolk and Suffolk. It may be found on waste ground and rubbish tips in various parts of Britain. Drooping Brome has been introduced into America and Australia as well as the British Isles.

61 Barren Brome
Bromus sterilis

Annual or biennial; culms 15–100 cm long, smooth. The leaves are hairy. The ligule is 2–4 mm long with a finely toothed margin. The panicle is spreading with long branches which are erect at first but later nodding. The spikelets are four- to ten-flowered, green or tinged with red, 4–6 cm long, including awns; the rough awn is considerably longer than the compressed, sharply-keeled lemma. Flowering period: May to July.

Barren Brome grows as a weed in open places and on waste ground. Despite the name, it produces viable seeds. The species is widely distributed in the British Isles, especially in the lowlands. Originally from Europe and western Asia, it has been introduced to North America and New Zealand.

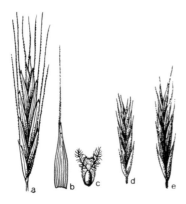

Barren Brome (61) – (a) spikelet, (b) lemma, (c) pistil. Spikelet (d) of Hairy or Wood Brome (62). Spikelet (e) of Upright Brome (63). (a, b, d and e natural size and c 5 × natural size.)

62 Hairy or Wood Brome
Bromus ramosus

A loosely tufted perennial; culms 45–190 cm long. The sheaths have long reflexed hairs and two auricles at the apex. The ligule is up to 6 mm long. The panicle is up to 45 cm long with spreading, nodding branches. The spikelets are 2·5–4 cm long, including awns, narrow, compressed, with four to eleven florets. The sharply-keeled lemma has an awn 4–8 mm long. Flowering period: July to August.

Hairy or Wood Brome grows in damp shady places in deci-duous woods and hedgerows, occasionally on roadsides and in formerly wooded areas. It is widespread throughout the British Isles except northern and central Scotland. It is common in Europe.

The closely related species Lesser Hairy Brome, *Bromus benekenii* grows in similar habitats and can be identified by the nearly smooth upper sheaths, the lower are slightly hairy.

63 Upright Brome
Bromus erectus

A perennial with dense tufts; culms 40–120 cm long, stiff, erect. The leaves are narrow and hairy at the margins; the ligule is up to 3 mm long, jagged. The erect or nodding panicles are purplish, reddish or green with erect or spreading branches. The compressed spikelets are 1·5–4 cm long. The keeled lemma has an awn 2–8 mm long. Flowering period: June to July.

This species is characteristic of dry, chalky downs, but is also found along roadsides and on waste ground. Upright Brome is common in southern England, local or rare in the rest of the British Isles. It is widespread in Europe, south-western Asia and north-western Africa.

has spread with cultivation to North and South America and Australia.

64 Soft Brome or Lop Grass
Bromus hordeaceus

A loosely tufted annual or biennial; culms 10–100 cm long, softly hairy, usually erect, sometimes prostrate. The leaves are softly hairy; the ligule is hairy and toothed. The panicle is erect and contracted after flowering. Spikelets oblong to ovate, six- to twelve-flowered. The lemmas are convex, awned, smooth or hairy. Flowering period: May to July.

Lop Grass is common throughout the British Isles, along roadsides, in meadows and on waste ground. A native of Europe and western Asia it

65 Field Brome
Bromus arvensis

A grey-green annual; culms 25–90 cm long. The blades are soft and limp, the lower sheaths softly hairy, the ligule is 2–4 mm long and jagged. The large, green or purplish, many-flowered panicle has long, thin branches which remain open after flowering. The spikelets are 10–20 mm long, smooth, oblong, four- to ten-flowered. The awn is the same length as the lemma. Flowering period: June to August.

An introduced species to Britain, and a rare plant of waste ground and rubbish dumps. At one time it was possibly cultivated for hay as it is on the Continent. Common throughout Europe and temperate Asia, it has also been introduced to North America.

66 Rye Brome
Bromus secalinus

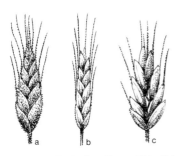

Spikelets of (a) *Lop Grass* (64), (b) *Field Brome* (65) *and* (c) *Rye Brome* (66) *with partly inrolled lower glumes.* (1½ × *natural size.*)

Annual or biennial; culms 20–120 cm long, stout, smooth. The leaves are hairy; the sheaths smooth; the ligule toothed. The panicle is erect, spreading during flowering and finally nodding. The smooth spikelets are 11–25 mm long, with four to eleven florets. The lemmas are overlapping, but later the edges become inrolled. The rough awn is fine and straight. The caryopsis is enclosed by the inrolled lemma and palea. Flowering period: June to July.

Rye Brome is an ancient weed probably introduced to Britain with cereal seeds. Formerly very common it sometimes appears as a weed in wheat fields and on waste ground, but is now much rarer due to the effective cleaning of cereal seed and improved land drainage in fields. Through cultivation, the species has spread over large areas of the world.

FALSE-BROME

The false-Brome Grasses, *Brachypodium*, are intermediate in structure between the Bromes and Couch-Grasses. They have long spikelets like those of Brome, but grouped in a spike-like raceme, rather than a panicle. The flat surface of the spikelets face the axis of the culm like Couch, but in False-Brome, at least some spikelets are shortly pedicelled rather than sessile.

67 Slender or Wood False-Brome
Brachypodium sylvaticum

A densely tufted perennial; culms 30–90 cm long, hairy at the nodes, otherwise smooth. The leaves are wide and drooping with a strong white central nerve below. The sheaths are hairy. The ligule is 1–6 mm long. The inflorescence is a spike-like, nodding raceme 6–20 cm long. The spikelets are cylindrical at first, later somewhat compressed with eight to sixteen florets. The upper spikelets are sessile, the lower shortly pedicelled. The glumes are short, less than half as long as the whole spikelet excluding the awn. The awn of the lemma is as long as the lemma itself. Flowering period: July to August.

Slender or Wood False-Brome grows on rich, peaty soil in woods and copses. The species is quite common in the fertile areas of the British Isles and is widespread throughout Europe, northern Africa and parts of Asia.

MARRAM

The Marram Grasses are closely related to the Small-Reeds, the most obvious differences between the two genera being in the inflorescence. The inflorescence of Marram is a compact cylindrical panicle with extremely short branches, that of the Small-Reed is a richly branched panicle with much longer branches.

68 Marram Grass
Ammophila arenaria

A coarse, pale greyish-green closely tufted perennial with long, branched rhizomes; culms 50–120 cm long. The leaves are stiff with pointed tips, smooth and convex below, ribbed above, the ribs with minute hairs. In dry weather the leaves are completely inrolled; the blades remain green throughout winter. The ligule is 1–3 cm long, narrow and pointed. The pale spike-like panicle is narrow with short erect branches. The spikelets are 10–16 mm long, one-flowered and closely overlapping. The glumes are longer than the lemmas and paleas. The lemma has a short fringe of hairs at the base and a small point near the tip. Flowering period: July to August.

Marram Grass is a most important plant in the initial stabilisation of sand dunes as it prevents sand erosion. Its long, branching rhizomes spread through the dunes holding the sand in place. As the rhizomes are covered in sand, they grow more strongly. The leaves and culms stand as scattered tufts on the bare white sand.

Marram Grass is common around the coast of the British Isles, often having been planted. It is also found along the western coast of Europe. Closely-related species are to be found along the Mediterranean coasts and along the east coast of North America.

Where Marram Grass grows with Wood Small-Reed or Bush Grass (15) they often form

Marram Grass (68) – (a) spikelet, (b) floret surrounded by the lemma and the palea. (3 × natural size.)

hybrids. The hybrid known as Baltic Marram Grass, *Ammocalamagrostis baltica* can be distinguished from Marram Grass by the larger, looser purplish panicle.

69   Lyme Grass
Elymus (*Leymus*) *arenarius*

A robust, bluish-green perennial with long, stout rhizomes; culms 60–200 cm long, stiff, erect. The leaves are 8–20 mm wide, somewhat inrolled with prominent ribs on the surface and stiff, pointed tips; at the apex of the sheath there are two narrow spreading auricles; the ligule is less than 1 mm long and has minute hairs at the margins. The inflorescence is a thick spike, up to 30 cm long, with pairs of spikelets at each node. The spikelets are three- to six-flowered. The glumes are nearly as long as the spikelet. The lemma is pointed, but has no awn. Flowering period: June to August.

Lyme Grass grows on sandy and stony shorelines and at the base of sand dunes. It has a high nutrient requirement and is normally found in the outer parts of the dunes where spume and washed up seaweed provide nourishment. It may be found on sandy roads further inland, spread by transport of sand and seaweed. The grass has occasionally been planted to fight sand erosion.

The species is common along the coasts of the British Isles and is found growing wild along the coasts of northern and north-western Europe and in other places in the world where it has been introduced by ships using beach sand as ballast.

Lyme Grass frequently grows in association with Marram Grass with which it is often confused. Lyme Grass is distinguished by the considerably wider leaves, the very short, blunt ligules and the three- to six-flowered spikelets.

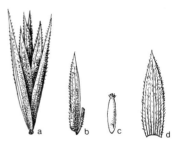

Lyme Grass (69) – (a) *spikelet with fertile florets and one small sterile floret at the top of the axis*, (b) *lemma surrounding the seed with a fragment of the axis at the base*, (c) *a ripe seed viewed from the dorsal side and* (d) *the lemma*, (1½ × *natural size*.)

70 Wood Barley

Hordelymus europaeus

A loosely tufted perennial; culms 40–120 cm long. The leaves are rough and fairly wide, hairy above and with a prominent, whitish central nerve below; the sheaths are covered with long, spreading or deflexed hairs, the upper hairless, the apices with short spreading auricles; the ligule is less than 1 mm long. The pale green spike is densely-flowered with three spikelets at each node, the trios alternating on opposite sides of the axis. The spikelets are one-flowered, the two lateral spikelets always bisexual, the central one either bisexual or male. Flower-ing period: June to July.

Wood Barley grows in woods and shady places, especially on lime-rich soil. It may form extensive stands, especially in beech woods. Fairly widespread from Wiltshire to Kent and northwards to Northumber-land. It is also widespread in Europe, Africa and Asia.

Wood Barley is often treated as a member of the Barley or Lyme Grass genera. It is distin-guished from the British species of Barley by the bisexual lateral spikelets which break up at maturity above the persistent glumes. It is distinguished from Lyme Grass by the tufted habit, single-flowered spikelets and the long awns of the glumes and lemmas.

BARLEY

The Barley genus, *Hordeum*, comprises spike-bearing grasses with single-flowered spikelets grouped in threes at each node of the axis. The central spikelet in each group contains a single bisexual floret, the two lateral spikelets male or sterile florets. One excep-tion is the six-rowed Barley (84), where each spikelet contains a bisexual floret. The glumes are very narrow and terminate in long awns; they do not enclose the spikelet, but are placed side by side below the lemmas which also terminate with long awns. The lemma and palea enclose the caryopsis through to maturity; they remain tightly attached to the caryopsis even after threshing. In wild species, the rhachis disarticulates when the seed is ripe. Each group of spikelets, each containing one seed, falls separately, complete with a piece of the rhachis. The long-awned glumes of the barren spikelets remain attached to the grain and presumably help in dispersal.

In cultivated species of Barley (83, 84), the rhachis does not disarticulate when the corn is ripe. These species are discussed later together with our other cereals.

The genus is comprised of twenty species, three of which are found wild in the British Isles.

71 Meadow Barley
Hordeum secalinum

A loosely tufted perennial; culms 20–80 cm long, slender. The inflorescence is a 2–8 cm long densely-flowered spike with comparatively short awns. The single-flowered spikelets are placed in threes, alternating on opposite sides of the axis. The glumes are extremely thin, nearly bristle-shaped and have no hairs at the margin. Flowering period: June to July.

Meadow Barley grows in coastal meadows and dykes, especially in the southern part of the British Isles. The grass is widespread in western and southern Europe and northern Africa.

72 Wall Barley
Hordeum murinum

A yellowish-green or reddish-tinged loosely tufted annual; culms 6–60 cm long. The upper

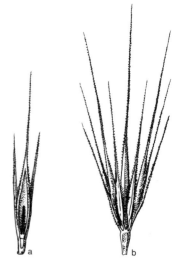

Wood Barley (70) – (a), a single-flowered spikelet surrounded by the two glumes and viewed from the ventral side. Note the rachilla at the front of the seed. Wall Barley (72) – (b) a group of three single-flowered spikelets viewed from the dorsal margin, sitting on a portion of the inflorescence axis. (2 × natural size.)

116

leaf-sheaths are inflated and often envelop the lowest portion of the spike. The spike is pale green with awns about 2 cm long, which are erect at first and later spreading. The glumes are narrow and lanceolate at the base where there are hairs along the margin. Flowering period: end of May to August.

Wall Barley is a plant of waste and disturbed ground, especially on waysides and near walls and buildings. The species is widely distributed in the British Isles, but uncommon in grassland and mountainous districts. It is found throughout Europe and south-western Asia.

Flowering period: June to August.

Mat-Grass is thought to be apomictic and able to set seeds without pollination. It grows on poor soil and is mainly found on heaths and sandy soils. As a fodder grass it is worthless, only being grazed in spring after which it becomes too tough. The species is widely distributed in the British Isles, but less frequent in the south-east. It is found over most of Europe, especially in mountain districts, in Asia, Africa, Greenland and Newfoundland.

73 Mat-Grass
Nardus stricta

A densely tufted perennial with short rhizomes, surrounded at the base by withered sheaths; culms 10–40 cm long, erect, stiff. The leaves are stiff, bristle-shaped and greyish-green. The inflorescence is a stiff, erect, narrow bluish-violet spike; the spikelets in two rows on the same side of the axis and depressed into it. The spikelets are single-flowered. The glumes are minute or absent. The single stigma is minutely hairy.

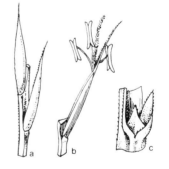

Mat-Grass (73) – (a) a portion of the spike with two one-flowered spikelets on the same side of the axis, (b) a flowering spikelet at anthesis and (c) a section of the axis of the inflorescence with the spikelet removed to reveal the outer glumes. (a 3 ×, b 4 × and c 10 × natural size.)

COUCH OR TWITCH

The species of Couch or Twitch, *Elymus*, are tufted, sometimes rhizomatous perennials. The inflorescence is a spike with a tough axis. The spikelets are solitary or in groups of two or three at each node, the flat side of the spikelet facing the axis. The spikelets have two to eleven florets. At maturity the rhachis may break up beneath each floret, or at the base of the spikelet, which then falls entire. The glumes are narrow, lanceolate and shorter than the spikelet. The lemma is lanceolate, with or without an awn. There are 110 species, four of which are British.

74 Bearded Couch
Elymus caninus

A loosely tufted perennial; culms 30–110 cm long. The leaves are fairly broad and reflexed; the apices of the sheaths have narrow auricles; the ligule is less than 1·5 mm long. The inflorescence is a slim, somewhat nodding spike. The spikelets are placed in two alternating rows on either side

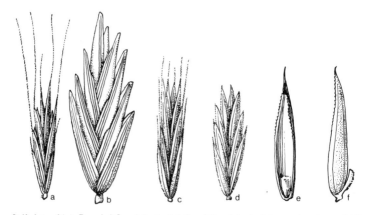

Spikelets of (a) *Bearded Couch* (*74*), (b) *Sand Couch* (*75*), (c) *awn-bearing and* (d) *awn-less varieties of Couch* (*76*). *A seed of Couch viewed from* (e) *the ventral and* (f) *the lateral sides.* (a–d *2* ×, e *and* f *3* × *natural size.*)

of the axis, the flat side towards the axis. The spikelets are 10–20 mm long, with two to six florets. The glumes are narrow with sharp points or sometimes short awns. The lemma has a long, straight or wavy awn, longer than the lemma itself. Flowering period: June to August.

Bearded Couch grows in woods and hedgerows and is widespread throughout England and Wales, but rare in the north of Scotland and Ireland. It is widespread throughout Europe and Asia.

75 Sand Couch
Elymus farctus ssp. *boreali-atlanticus*

A bluish-grey perennial with creeping rhizomes; culms 20–60 cm long. The spreading or drooping leaves are flat, inrolled in dry weather, smooth below, ribbed above, the ribs densely and minutely hairy. The sheath is without auricles; the ligule is 0·5–1 mm long. The inflorescence is an erect or curved spike, the spikelets placed in alternate rows on the axis, flat sides towards the axis. The spike is very brittle, easily breaking just above each spikelet. The spikelets are 15–28 mm long with three to eight florets. Flowering period: June to August.

Sand Couch grows on sandy shorelines, often amongst Lyme Grass (69) and Marram Grass (68). Its high tolerance of salt allows it to form low dunes farther down the shore than any other British grass. It is common on sandy coastal areas of the British Isles and Europe and it has been introduced to North America.

Where Sand Couch grows with Couch or Twitch, the two species may hybridise. Sand Couch may be distinguished from both Couch and the hybrid by the densely hairy ribs on the upper leaf surface, the brittle spikes and the fertile anthers.

76 Couch or Twitch
Elymus repens

A fresh green, or bluish-green, perennial with wiry rhizomes, giving rise to scattered tufts with numerous sterile shoots; culms 30–120 cm long. The leaves are flat, 3–10 mm wide with sparse long hairs on the upper surface. At the apex of the sheath are two short, spreading auricles; the ligule is less than 1 mm long. The inflorescence is an erect spike with packed spikelets. The spikelets are 10–20 mm long with three to eight florets. The glumes are shorter than the spikelet. The lemma is lanceolate, blunt or sharply pointed at the tip, rarely with a short awn. Flowering period: June to August.

Couch or Twitch is one of our most common and pernicious weeds, appearing everywhere except in the poorest soil. Every broken piece of a rhizome is capable of growing into a new plant. The rhizomes are nutritious and when washed can be used as fodder for animals. They have also been used as a blood-cleansing cure in folk medicine. It originated in Europe and western Asia, but with cultivation has spread to the temperate regions of the Northern and Southern Hemispheres.

RYE GRASS

The species of Rye Grass, *Lolium* are spike-bearing grasses with compressed, many-flowered spikelets. These occur in alternating rows on the rhachis, the narrow edges towards the axis. Apart from the upper spikelet, the remainder have only one glume, on the side away from the rhachis. In some species the glume is longer than the spikelet, in others it is shorter. The seed is invested by the lemma and palea, even when dispersed at maturity. A small portion of the rhachis remains attached to the base of each seed. There are about six species, of which three occur in Britain.

77 Perennial Rye-Grass
Lolium perenne

A loosely tufted perennial with numerous sterile shoots; culms 10–90 cm long, smooth, noded at the base. The leaves are shiny and smooth with a distinct keel on the underside. At the apex of the leaf-sheath are two narrow auricles, though sometimes absent on weak shoots; the ligule is short. The spike is 4–30 cm long, green or reddish-tinged. The spikelet is 7–20 mm long with four to fourteen florets. The glume is considerably shorter than the spikelet. The lemma and palea are usually without awns. Flowering period: May to August.

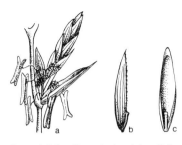

Perennial Rye-Grass (77) – (a) spikelet at the beginning of the flowering period with part of the inflorescence axis. A seed of the same species viewed from (b) the lateral and (c) the ventral sides. (a 2 ×, b and c 3 × natural size.)

Perennial Rye-Grass is one of our best fodder grasses, suitable for both hay and grazing and has been cultivated in Britain for at least the last 300 years. It is most often grown in a mixture with clover or other species of grass. It is very tolerant of wear and tear so is ideal for sports grounds and lawns. It thrives on damp, rich soil, but may also appear on roadsides and in waste places throughout Britain. It probably originated in Europe and western Asia, but through cultivation has spread throughout the world.

78 Italian Rye-Grass
Lolium multiflorum

A loosely tufted annual or biennial; culms 30–100 cm long, rough towards the spike. The spikelets are five- to fifteen-flowered. The glume is less than half the length of the spikelet. The lemma has a fine, straight awn as long as the lemma itself. Flowering period: June to August.

Italian Rye-Grass is a native of central and southern Europe and western Asia. It has been cultivated as a fodder plant in the British Isles since 1830, especially to obtain rapid results and good growth in the first year. It is often found naturalised on roadsides and is now widespread from cultivation both in the Northern and Southern Hemispheres.

79 Darnel
Lolium temulentum

An annual without sterile shoots; culms 30–90 long, stiff, erect, often branched from the base. The glume is the same length as the spikelet. The lemma usually has a long awn. Flowering period: June to August.

Darnel is an ancient field weed, though now it is restricted to wasteland and rubbish dumps. The species is regarded as native to western Asia, but with cereal production, has spread throughout the world.

The seeds of Darnel sometimes contain a parasitic fungus, *Endoconidium temulentum* which produces a poisonous alkaloid, temuline.

80 Sea Hard-Grass
Parapholis strigosa

A bluish-green annual; culms 5–40 cm long, curved, erect, branched from the base. The inrolled leaves are short and bristle-shaped, the inflorescence is a stiff, erect or slightly curved spike, little thicker than the culm itself. The spikelets are embedded in hollows in the spike-axis, alternating in two rows up the axis. The spikelets are single-flowered. Flowering period: June to August.

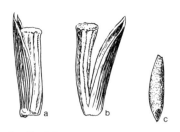

Sea Hard-Grass (80) –(a) and (b) part of the inflorescence axis each with a one-flowered spikelet, containing a mature seed. A seed (c) as seen from the dorsal surface. (5 × natural size.)

Sea Hard-Grass grows along the coasts of the British Isles, but is easily overlooked since the thin, pointed spikes are rather insignificant. The species is found as far north as Lothian and the Isle of Mull. It is distributed along the west coasts of Europe from Scotland to Portugal.

81 Bread Wheat
Triticum aestivum

An annual; culms 60–120 cm long. The leaf-sheaths are softly hairy and have two prominent auricles at the apex. The leaf-blades are flat and softly hairy like the sheaths; the ligule is short and blunt. The inflorescence is usually a dense, sometimes quadrangular spike. The somewhat compressed spikelets are borne alternately on the rhachis, the flat side of each spikelet, towards the axis. The spikelets contain three to five hermaphrodite florets. The glumes are ovate, convex and keeled in the upper half. The lemma is ovate and may or may not be equipped with an awn. The caryopsis is only loosely enveloped by the lemma and palea. Flowering period: June to July.

Spikelet of Bread Wheat (81). (2 × natural size.) See also page 13.

Bread Wheat is the most highly developed and widely grown of all wheats. It has many thousands of cultivars, mostly developed by breeding. This species is self-pollinating, the glumes remaining closed. Cross-fertilisation is artificial. There are winter, spring and intermediate varieties, in awned and awnless forms. The spike is usually long in proportion to its width, although dense, square-head types (ssp. *compactum*) are not uncommon. The grains may be a variety of colours from white through red to purple. For strong growth, wheat requires a rich soil. Grown wherever conditions are suitable, wheat is only found in cultivated fields, through occasional plants may occur where grain has been accidentally spilled.

82 Rye
Secale cereale

Annual or occasionally perennial; culms 50–150 cm long. Leaves blue-green usually finely hairy; the leaf-sheaths are often reddish-brown, the apex with two large auricles encircling the culm, the ligule is up to 3 mm long. The inflorescence is a loose spike, the spikelets in two alternating rows up the axis, the terminal spikelet absent. The spikelets have three florets, the two lower hermaphrodite, the upper sterile. The glumes are narrow and pointed. The

Flowering spikelet of Rye (82). Due to lack of space, the awns have been cut off. Between the two fertile florets there is a rudimentary floret at the apex of the rachilla. (3 × natural size.)

lemma is sharply-keeled and awnless. The ripe caryopsis is pointed at the base, somewhat wrinkled, with an apical hairy tuft. Flowering period: approximately June to September.

Rye is usually grown on poor soil where other crops are unsuccessful. It survives the cold well, and is usually wintersown. It is cultivated throughout the cool temperate regions of the world.

A number of varieties of Rye are known but the variation is so great that their identification is very difficult.

BARLEY

The wild species of Barley have been described earlier (70–72). The cultivated species differ from the wild species by having a tough rhachis which does not break up at maturity.

83 Two-Rowed Barley
Hordeum distichon

An annual; culms 50–90 cm long. The leaves are pale green; the sheaths have two smooth spreading auricles at the apex. The rhachis of the spike is tough and bearded at the margin. The spikelets are grouped in threes, in two alternating rows along the rhachis. The spikelet has three florets, the two lateral male or sterile, the central hermaphrodite. The fertile lemma has a long awn. Flowering period: June.

Two-Rowed Barley is widely cultivated in temperate and subtropical areas. In Britain it is grown as a spring-sown crop.

84 Six-Rowed Barley
Hordeum vulgare

Similar to Two-Rowed Barley but distinguished by the spike-

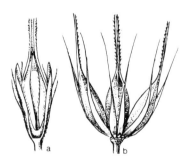

Spikelets of (a) *Two-Rowed Barley (83) and* (b) *Six-Rowed Barley (84). Due to lack of space the awns have been cut off.* (2 × *natural size.*)

lets in which all three florets are hermaphrodite and viable. The lemmas all bear long, stout awns. Flowering period: June to September.

Six-Rowed Barley is more hardy and has a wider range than Two-Rowed Barley. In Britain it is sown as both a winter and spring crop.

85 Oats
Avena sativa

An annual; culms 50–180 cm long, erect, sometimes prostrate at the base. Leaves green or glaucous; the blades finely pointed, flat and rough; the ligules are fairly long and pointed. The panicles are erect, nodding, with fine, spreading branches. The spikelets are 1·7–5 cm long (excluding awns) with one to seven florets; the rhachis is persistent at maturity. The glumes are equal or slightly unequal, as long as the spikelet. The lemma has two unequal points at the tip; the awn (if present) is attached at the middle of the lemma and does not exceed the tip. The palea has a hairy keel and may be prickly on the back. Flowering period: April to November.

Oats are a very important cereal crop and have been

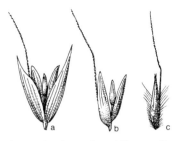

An awn-bearing variety of Common Oat (85) – (a) spikelet, (b) two fertile florets and a sterile floret removed from the outer glumes but still surrounded by the lemma and palea. Floret (c) of Bristle Oat (86). (Natural size.)

subjected to many breeding trials. This has resulted in the production of a large number of cultivars which pose problems of identification.

Common Oat is widely cultivated in the temperate belts of both hemispheres. It may also occur as a weed on roadsides, disturbed ground and in cereal fields. Common Oat requires more humid conditions than wheat and barley, but tolerates poorer soil.

A second species, Bristle or Small Oat, *Avena fatua* (86), is cultivated in mountainous districts of the British Isles. It may be distinguished from Common Oats by the presence of two bristles at the tip of the lemma.

Seeds of four cereal species viewed from the dorsal and ventral surfaces – (a) *and* (b) *Bread Wheat,* (c) *and* (d) *Rye,* (e) *and* (f) *Common Oat,* (g) *and* (h) *Two-Rowed Barley. (2 × natural size.)*

    In Wheat and Rye, the seeds are 'naked', i.e. not enclosed in the palea and lemma. The embryo can easily be seen through the base at the back of the seed. Wheat has a plump seed, with a smooth surface. Rye, by contrast, has a narrow seed with a wrinkled surface.

    The seeds of Oats and Barley are enveloped in the palea. In Barley, the palea merges with the seed-wall, whereas in Oats, it can be separated from the seed coat.

Maize
Zea mays

A robust annual; culms up to 4, sometimes 9 metres long, solid, with prop roots developing from the lower nodes. The leaves are 3–15 cm wide, undulate. The male inflorescence is a terminal panicle of spike-like racemes with the spikelets arranged in pairs; one spikelet is sessile, the other is stalked. The female inflorescences (corn-cobs) are borne in the axils of the leaves; the spikelets occur as longitudinal rows on a thickened axis, and enclosed by a number of modified leaf-sheaths. The male spikelets have two florets; the female spikelets also have two florets, the lower usually sterile. The female floret has a single long style. The seeds may be variously coloured, from white through red to purple. Flowering period: July to October.

Maize is an unusual grass in being monoecious, that is having male and female florets on the same plant. The modified leaf-sheaths which envelop the female inflorescences are unique to Maize.

Maize is cultivated throughout the world, wherever conditions permit. In Britain it is usually grown as a green fodder crop, though increasingly as a

  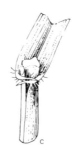 

Identification of cereal grasses in their vegetative state can be determined by the appearance of the base of the leaf-blade.

In Oats (a) *the base of the blade is entirely without auricles.*

In Barley (b) *the hairless auricles are long and sickle-shaped and wrap around the culm.*

Wheat (c), *too, has well-developed auricles, but these are hairy at the edges.*

Rye (d) *has rather short, narrow auricles, without hairs. This species is also recognised by the blue-green colour of the leaves. The sheath is often hairy and the ligule is very short, only 1 mm long.*

vegetable and occasionally for ornament.

87 Common or Broom-Corn Millet
Panicum miliaceum

An annual; culms 30–100 cm long. The leaves are broad; the sheaths long haired; the ligule is a ring of silky hairs. The inflorescence is a richly branched, somewhat nodding panicle. The spikelets are compressed dorsally, and have two florets; the tiny lower floret is male or sterile, the upper floret hermaphrodite. The glumes are un-equal, the larger ½–⅔ as long as the spikelet, the smaller is shorter and many-veined. The lemma of the lower floret resembles the shorter glume and has no palea. The lemma and palea of the upper floret envelop the mature caryopsis. Flowering period: July to October.

Common Millet is an ancient cultivated plant, thought to have originated in central Asia. It is a rare alien in the British Isles, found on rubbish dumps and usually growing from seeds thrown away with the rubbish from bird cages.

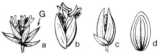

Common Millet (87) –(a) *flowering spikelet*, (b) *fertile floret enclosed in the lemma and palea*, (c) *seed apparently surrounded by three scales, but the uppermost of these is the lemma of a sterile floret*, (d) *ripe seed enveloped in the shiny, hard palea*. (a *2* × , b, c *and* d *3* × *natural size*.)

florets, the upper hermaphrodite, the lower represented only by a lemma and minute palea. One glume is absent or very minute, the other is as long as the spikelet and minutely hairy. The lemma of the lower floret is similar to the glume; that of the upper floret is brownish and smooth. Flowering period: August to September.

Smooth Finger-Grass is a native of warm temperate Europe and Asia. A rare grass in southern and south-eastern England, it may be found in sandy fields and occasionally on waste ground and rubbish dumps near ports and railways.

Maize.
(*Reduced in size.*)

88 Smooth Finger-Grass
Digitaria ischaemum

A delicate annual; culms 10–35 cm long, smooth, prostrate, then ascending, branched from the base. The inflorescence is composed of two to eight spike-like, one-sided racemes grouped at or near top of the culm. The small, oval spikelets have unequal pedicels. The spikelets have two

89 Cockspur Grass
Echinochloa crus-galli

An annual; culms 30–120 cm long. The leaves are broad, smooth, and rough at the edges;

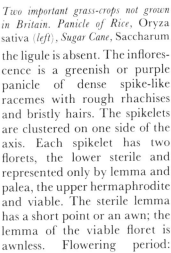

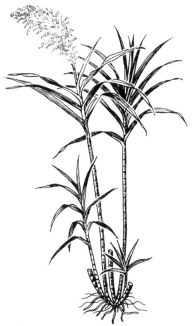

Two important grass-crops not grown in Britain. Panicle of Rice, Oryza sativa (*left*), *Sugar Cane,* Saccharum officinarum (*right*). (*Both reduced in size.*)

the ligule is absent. The inflorescence is a greenish or purple panicle of dense spike-like racemes with rough rhachises and bristly hairs. The spikelets are clustered on one side of the axis. Each spikelet has two florets, the lower sterile and represented only by lemma and palea, the upper hermaphrodite and viable. The sterile lemma has a short point or an awn; the lemma of the viable floret is awnless. Flowering period: August to October.

Cockspur Grass is an uncommon alien in the British Isles; appearing on cultivated and waste ground. A North American species it has spread to temperate and tropical regions through cultivation.

Cockspur Grass is a variable species, some forms having long awned spikelets, some awnless spikelets and some awned and awnless spikelets mixed in the same panicle.

90   Green Bristle-Grass
Setaria viridis

A loosely tufted annual; culms 10–60 cm long. The leaves are lanceolate and rough; the ligule is a ring of silky hairs. The inflorescence is a spike-like panicle, 1–10 cm long, green or reddish-tinged, with one to three rough bristles beneath each spikelet. The spikelets are blunt, oval with two florets, the upper viable, the lower represented only by a lemma and palea. The glumes are unequal, the lower about ⅓ the length of the spikelet, one- to three-nerved, the upper as long as the spikelet, five-nerved. The sterile lemma is similar to the upper glume, five- to seven-nerved, the upper lemma is smaller and becomes tough and wrinkled. The caryopsis is tightly enclosed by the lemma and palea. Flowering period: August to October.

A rather rare weed in Britain, occurring on cultivated and waste ground, especially in the south. Originally a native of temperate Europe and Asia, Green Bristle-Grass has spread through the temperate regions of the world due to cultivation.

This is a variable species, especially with regard to the shape and size of the panicles and the colour of the seeds.

91   Italian Millet or Fox-Tail
Setaria italica

A robust annual; culms 100 cm long. Panicle long, richly branched, bristly, somewhat nodding. Flowering period: July to October.

Italian Millet is cultivated in warm, temperate countries as a source of bird seed. In Britain it is sometimes found on rubbish dumps, growing from discarded seed.

Italian Millet is a derivative of Green Bristle-Grass and is very similar to that species. Italian Millet is distinguished by the longer panicle and by the upper floret falling from the remainder of the spikelet at maturity.

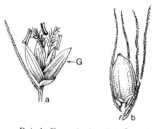

Green Bristle Grass (90) – (a) flowering spikelet, (b) spikelet surrounded by rough bristles (stems of sterile spikelets). (4 × natural size.)

92 Townsend's Cord-Grass
Spartina townsendii

A robust perennial with short, thick rhizomes; culms 30–130 cm long, erect. The leaves are stiff, flat or inrolled and ribbed above; the ligule is a dense fringe of hairs 1–2 mm long. The inflorescence is a long, narrow panicle of two to nine erect spikes. The compressed single-flowered spikelets are closely overlapping, placed in two rows along one side of the spike and compressed against the axis. Flowering period: July to September.

Townsend's Cord-Grass is found in scattered localities around the coasts of Britain and Ireland, especially along the south coast from Dorset to Sussex. It is also known in France and Denmark.

It is almost certain that Townsend's Cord-Grass is a natural hybrid between Smooth Cord-Grass, *Spartina alterniflora* and Cord-Grass, *Spartina maritima*. It first appeared in Britain on the shores of Southampton Water and has since spread slowly along the coast. Townsend's Cord-Grass is a sterile hybrid, new colonies being established by whole plants or rhizomes being uprooted and washed to new sites. By a doubling of the chromosomes Townsend's Cord-Grass has given rise to the fertile species Common Cord-Grass, *Spartina anglica*, from which it may be distinguished by the narrower upper leaf-blades, shorter ligular hairs and wider, more hairy spikelets.

THE SEDGE FAMILY – CYPERACEAE

93 Brown Cyperus
Cyperus fuscus

A small tufted annual; stems 3–12 cm long, triangular, bearing narrow leaves, which wither early. The inflorescence, surrounded by three long narrow bracts is a compact dark brown head or umbel. The spikelets are 3–5 mm long, with boat-shaped glumes placed in two rows along the axis of the spikelet, the florets are bisexual and consist of two stamens and an ovary with three feather-shaped stigmas at the end of a short style. The fruit is a three-sided nut. Flowering period: July to September.

Brown Cyperus grows on the damp margins of ponds and lakes. The seeds can remain

Brown Cyperus (93) – (a) spikelet, (b) floret in the axis of the boat-shaped glume, (c) nut. (a 5 ×, b 9 × and c 12 × natural size.)

Bog Rush (94) – (a) spikelet, (b) floret, (c) nut, surrounded by the rough persistent perianth bristles. (a 1½ ×, b 4 × and c 6 × natural size.)

viable for a decade or more and germinate only in warm, dry summers. The plant is extremely rare in Great Britain, restricted to southern England. The sedge is widespread in central and southern Europe, northern Africa and Asia with rare appearances in Scandinavia.

94 Bog Rush
Schoenus nigricans

A perennial growing in dense tufts. Stems 15–75 cm long which are thin and stiff, and are invested at the base by shiny brown sheaths with short, bristle-shaped blades. The inflorescence is a terminal, narrow, spindle-shaped rust-coloured head composed of two to three spikelets, surrounded by a couple of narrow bracts, which are no longer than the inflorescence itself. The spikelets are two-rowed and contain three to four flowers. The floret is bisexual and has a much reduced perianth, which consists of up to six rough bristles, with three stamens and an ovary with three stigmas at the tip. The fruit is a three-sided nut. Flowering period: May to June.

Bog Rush grows in marshes. It is quite widespread in Great Britain.

95 White Beak-Sedge
Rhynchospora alba

A perennial sedge occurring in sparse tufts. The delicate stems are 20–30 cm long. The leaves are narrow and distinctly channelled. The inflorescence consists of whitish, ultimately buff-coloured heads, composed

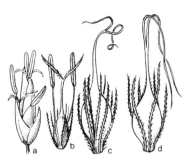

White Beak-Sedge (95) – (a) spikelet, (b) flower, (c) nut, surrounded by downward projected barbs on spiny perianth bristles. Brown Beak-Sedge (96) (d) nut surrounded by upward projecting barbs on perianth bristles. (a 3 × , b 4 × , c and d 10 × natural size.)

of clusters of small, cylindrical, two-flowered spikelets. The lower glumes in the spikelet are sterile and shorter than the others. The florets have much reduced perianths consisting of nine to thirteen barbed bristles, there are two to three stamens and an ovary, with a style bearing two stigmas. The fruit is a nut. At maturity, the style is swollen and remains as a pointed beak on the fruit. Flowering period: June to July.

White Beak-Sedge grows on poor wet acid soil or peat.

The species is local but scattered throughout the British Isles. It is widespread through-out the temperate zones of Europe and Asia.

96 Brown Beak-Sedge
Rhynchospora fusca

Similar to 95, but distinguished by the long horizontal rhizomes with long runners and much shorter stems, only 10–20 cm long, the long, dark reddish-brown flower heads, with an overtopping bract and florets with five or six perianth bristles and upward projecting barbs. Flowering period: July to August.

Brown Beak-Sedge grows in similar places as 95 but is much rarer and more localised. It occurs in much of Europe.

97 Common Spike-Rush
Eleocharis palustris

A tufted perennial plant with far creeping horizontal rhizomes; stems 10–60 cm long, cylindrical, rush-like, invested at the base by a couple of reddish-brown sheaths with no blades, but are otherwise leaf-less. Spikelets cylindrical 0·5–2 cm long, many-flowered; lowest glume not more than $\frac{1}{2}$ encircling its base; others ovate, margins hyaline. The florets are bisexual, the perianth reduced

Common Spike-Rush (97) – (a) *spikelet with the majority of the flowers at anthesis, with prominent anthers; only the upper flowers are still female receptive,* (b) *a single floret,* (c) *a ripe nut, surrounded by the persistent, rough bristles of the perianth.* (a *natural size,* b 2 × *and* c 5 × *natural size.*)

to a few, thin bristles. There are three stamens and the ovary has a long style with two stigmas. The fruit is a nut. At maturity, the lower portion of the style remains attached to the fruit as a defined beak. Flowering period: May to July.

Common Spike-Rush grows in marshes, ditches and at margins of ponds.

The species is common throughout the British Isles and throughout temperate parts of the World.

One-Glumed Spike-Rush
Eleocharis uniglumis

Similar to the previous species, but the stems are usually shiny,

the lower sheaths are reddish and the lowest glume entirely encircles the base of the spikelet. Flowering period: June to August.

It grows mainly in marshes near the coast, local inland. The species is widespread in Europe, northern Africa and western Asia.

98　Few-Flowered Spike-Rush
Eleocharis quinqueflora

A perennial; stems delicate 5–30 cm long, cylindrical, arranged in loose tufts. The base of the stems are invested with reddish-brown leaf-sheaths but are otherwise leafless. The inflorescence is a single terminal, few-flowered spike, 5–7 mm long, with the lowest glume encircling its base, others about 5 mm, ovate, acuminate reddish-brown with broad, hyaline margins. Each floret has a bristle-shaped perianth, three stamens and an ovary with a long style and three stigmas. Flowering period: June to July.

The Few-Flowered Spike-Rush grows on damp, rich, grassy soil at pond margins, and on moors and fenland with calcareous ground water.

The species is found locally

throughout the British Isles. It occurs throughout the Northern Hemisphere in temperate regions.

99 Bristle Scirpus
Scirpus setaceus

A small short-lived perennial or annual sedge; with stems 5–15 cm long, thread-like, forming close, round tufts. The stems bear two small, thread-like channelled leaves from the base. The inflorescence is solitary or in two or three oval spikelets up to 5 mm long, apparently placed just below the tip of the stem, because of the stem-like bracts which are a prolongation of the stem itself. The purplish-brown glumes have green mid-ribs and whitish margins. The florets have no perianth and have two stamens and one style with three stigmas. Flowering period: May to July.

Bristle Scirpus grows on open, damp, sandy or gravelly soil, e.g. at the edges of ponds and on damp heaths and sometimes in marshy meadows. The plant is found over the whole of the British Isles, but is rather local. The species is widespread in Europe, Asia, northern and southern Africa and Australia.

100 Broad Blysmus
Blysmus compressus

A perennial with far-creeping rhizomes; stems 10–35 cm long, slightly triangular, smooth. Leaves long, narrow, flat and sharply-keeled with rough edges. Inflorescence a composite compressed spike up to 2 cm long, consisting of ten to twelve reddish-brown spikelets, which are arranged in two opposite rows. Each spikelet contains six to eight bisexual flowers each subtended by a pointed brown glume. The floret has a bristle-shaped perianth, three stamens and an ovary with a long style and two stigmas. Flowering period: June to July.

Broad Blysmus grows in open damp, marsh meadows and occasionally in salt-marsh meadows. It is found especially on rich soil and is particularly common on well-trodden paths. The species is locally abundant throughout the British Isles and widespread throughout most of Europe and the temperate zones of Asia.

101 Wood Club-Rush
Scirpus sylvaticus

A stout perennial with horizontal, creeping rhizomes; stems

30–100 cm long, triangular at the top. The leaves are long, broad and pale green. The inflorescence is richly branched, consisting of brownish-green spikelets, 3–4 mm long, which are either solitary or in small groups.

The florets have six rough perianth bristles, three stamens and three stigmas. The flower is protogynous, i.e. the stigmas are receptive before anthesis. At the female phase the branches of the inflorescence are shorter and less widespread than they are in the male phase, as shown on the colour plate. Flowering period: June to July.

It grows on rich damp soil in marshes, wet places in woods, beside streams and in meadows where there is rising ground water. The plant is locally common in fertile areas of the British Isles and is widespread in the temperate zones of the Northern Hemisphere.

102   Deer Grass
Scirpus cespitosus

A densely tufted perennial; with stems 5–30 cm long, stiff cylindrical and smooth. The stem bases are invested with shiny, brown leaf-sheaths. The leaves have a short needle-shaped blade. The inflorescence is a solitary, terminal pale brown, few-flowered spike. The two larger lowest glumes have a long apical spikelet. Flowering period: May to June.

Deer Grass grows on damp, acid soil and is common on the marshy parts of heaths, mountains and moorlands throughout most of Britain. It is widespread in the temperate regions of the Northern Hemisphere. Two subspecies occur, Northern Deer Grass subspecies *cespitosus* and Western Deer Grass subspecies *germanicus*, the latter most common in the British Isles.

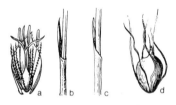

Wood Club-Rush (101) – (a) floret in the glume axis. Junction of the blade and the sheath on the uppermost stem leaf of the two varieties of Deer Grass (102), (b) the Northern Deer Grass, (c) Western Deer Grass. Nut (d) of Deer Grass, surrounded by the persistent perianth bristles. (a 6 ×, b and c 2 × and d 6 × natural size.)

103 Bulrush
Scirpus lacustris

A stout perennial; 1–3 m tall, with thick creeping rhizomes, stems numerous, dark green, cylindrical up to 1·5 cm thick, often leafless. The leaves usually consist of sheaths below, but with a short blade above. The inflorescence is a branched panicle, comprised of oval, reddish-brown spikelets, 5–8 mm long. It is apparently laterally placed, but is subtended by stem-like bracts. The glumes are oval, with a prominent mid-rib and often fringed. The florets are bisexual and have six perianth bristles, three stamens and three stigmas. Flowering period: June to July.

Bulrush and Common Reed-Grass (29) form dense stands in ponds and at the edges of slow-moving rivers and streams. The plant grows in water up to 2 metres in depth – deeper than Common Reed-Grass.

At the bottom of some lakes, Bulrush occasionally forms underwater meadows. The stems do not appear above the water level and never flower and curiously enough, submerged plants have well-developed leaf-blades. Bulrush can also grow on the coast, particularly in brackish water. The species is common throughout the British Isles, is widespread throughout the whole of the Northern Hemisphere and is also found in Australia and the South Sea Islands. The name Bulrush alludes to the fact that the thick soft, pith-filled stems are used for weaving rush mats, etc.

104 Sea Club-Rush
Scirpus maritimus

A stout perennial, with horizontal rhizomes which have bulbous swellings at the point where they bend upwards and form erect shoots; stems 30–100 cm long, smooth and distinctly triangular for the whole of their length. The leaves are narrow and have rough margins, and are sharply-keeled. The composite inflorescence is about 5 mm long and consists of large reddish-brown spikelets, which are grouped in tight glomerules, some of which are long-stemmed, others which are practically sessile. The inflorescence is invested with long leaf-like bracts. Flowering period: July to August.

Sea Club-Rush grows in close stands in shallow water at the

muddy margins of tidal rivers, ditches and ponds near the sea. It can form salt-reed swamps either alone or with Common Reed-Grass (29). The species is widespread in Britain and throughout most of the World.

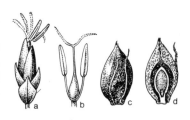

105 Saw Sedge
Cladium mariscus

A tough stout perennial with horizontal, creeping rhizomes; stems 1–2 m long, stiff, cylindrical or bluntly triangular, hollow. The leaves are long and stiff, 1·5 cm wide, evergreen, have a keel on the outer surface and are provided with small sharp teeth at the margins and on the keel. The inflorescence is a much-branched and rust-coloured panicle, each branch with three to ten spikelets. The spikelets are 3–4 mm long, reddish-brown, one- to three-flowered; the two to three lower glumes are sterile, the remainder fertile; the florets lack perianth bristles and usually have two stamens, an ovary with a long style and two or three stigmas, although the uppermost floret is sometimes male. The fruit is a nut. Flowering period: July to August.

Saw Sedge can form large stands at the edges of reed swamps and fens on neutral or alkaline soils. Locally abundant in the British Isles and widespread in temperate regions of the world. It is used as a thatching material in East Anglia.

COTTON GRASS

The genus *Eriophorum* includes many perennial sedges with bisexual flowers grouped in solitary or umbellate many-flowered spikes. The glumes are large, membranous and spirally arranged. The perianth segments elongate greatly after flowering to give a cotton wool appearance to the inflorescence. There are about twenty species of which two commonly occur in Britain.

106 Common Cotton-Grass
Eriophorum angustifolium

A perennial, with far-creeping horizontal rhizomes; stems 20–60 cm long, erect, cylindrical. Leaf-blades triangular in cross-section, in the upper half, and gulley-shaped in the lower half. Spikelets three to seven, the glumes about 7 mm long, one-nerved, lanceolate, pointed with a thin white margin. During the flowering period, the perianth bristles are hidden amongst the silvery-grey membranous glumes and at maturity grow to about 4 cm long.

Common Cotton-Grass grows in wet acid places such as bogs and pools in peaty marshes. The species is recorded in most districts of the British Isles and is also widespread throughout the Northern Hemisphere both in lowland and mountainous areas.

Common Cotton-Grass was once used to stuff pillows, but the hairs are not suitable for spinning since they are too brittle.

107 Hares-Tail
Eriophorum vaginatum

A densely tufted perennial with many stems 30–50 cm long. The

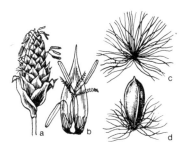

Hares-Tail (107) – (a) flowering spikelet, (b) floret in the glume axis, (c) a single fruit surrounded by long, silky wool, (d) the same with the hairs removed at the base to reveal the black three cornered nut. (a $1\frac{1}{2}$ ×, b 3 ×, c $\frac{2}{3}$ × and d 7 × natural size.)

radical leaves are long and bristle-shaped, and develop a year before flowering, the upper sheaths are strongly inflated but narrowed at the mouth. The inflorescence is a single terminal ovoid spike, rounded at the base. Glumes about 7 mm long, one-nerved ovate-lanceolate, acuminate, silvery below, slaty-black above. Flowering period: April to May.

Hares-Tail grows on damp peaty soil both on heaths and mountain heaths, where it often grows in large quantities. The plant does not require as much moisture as other cotton grasses and the marshes in which it grows often dry out on the surface during the summer.

The plant is distributed locally throughout most of the British Isles, but occurs most often in the north. It is also widespread throughout the Northern Hemisphere both in lowland and mountainous areas.

CAREX

The large genus *Carex* with 1,800 species throughout the world is well represented in the British Isles with about seventy species found in the native flora.

As can be seen from the colour plates, *Carex* species have a characteristic growth habit. British species are all perennial occurring either as tufts or with runners and scattered stems. The stems are pith-filled and triangular. They are invested by open sheaths which bear narrow, grass-like leaves, which are placed in three rows up the stem; the ligule is small. The colour and structure of the sheath can be a good guide to the identification.

By contrast to other genera the spikelets of *Carex* are always unisexual. The males consist of three stamens, placed in a very small floral receptacle in the corner of the glume. The perianth is absent. The female perianth is the utricle and it represents the first leaf on the axis of the female flowering shoot, the radical 'leaf'. In sedges, this 'leaf' is apparently formed by the fusion of two small leaves and therefore has two well-developed nerves, corresponding to the mid-ribs of the two leaves, but in *Carex* a further fusion has taken place, so that the radical leaf has become bottle-shaped.

The 'female flower' is a flowering side shoot, which extends from the corner of a glume on the axis of the inflorescence. This scale (glume) cannot be likened immediately to the glumes of the male flower, which actually support a flower.

The female flower is completely naked and simply consists of an ovary with a style and two or three stigmas.

The female flower can be considered to be a single-flowered inflorescence of complicated, reduced structures, a 'spikelet', but one which cannot be immediately compared with the spikelets of other sedges or grasses.

Species of *Carex*, as already mentioned, have a very uniform basic floral structure but are very variable in the way that the male and female flowers are grouped in the inflorescence. The genus *Carex* can be divided into two artificial groups, according to the type of the inflorescence to be found.

Group 1: THE SINGLE-SPIKED species (108–109) have only a single, terminal, spike-like inflorescence. Usually both sexes are found on the same spike (monoecious) with the male flowers uppermost and female flowers below. However, in certain species, e.g. Dioecious Sedge (108), the male and female flowers occur on different plants.

Group 2: THE PANICULATE group (110–121) includes species having several identical spike-like inflorescences which each contain both male and female flowers. In some species within each spikelet the male flowers are uppermost and the female flowers below, whilst in others, the reverse can occur. In some species, e.g. Sand Sedge (112), the upper spikelets are wholly male, the middle ones male above and female below and the lower spikelets entirely female.

The identification of *Carex* can only be adequately carried out with ripe fruiting material since most diagnostic features reside in the mature spikelet. When collecting species of *Carex*, one should note whether the stems grow in tufts, or have runners and are scattered.

108 Dioecious Sedge
Carex dioica

Tufted perennial with short erect rhizomes; stems 5–30 cm long, with narrow, bristle-shaped leaves emerging from the base. The terminal spike-like inflorescences are either solely male or female. The male spikes are pale brown and quite small. The female spikelets bear oval utricles 2·5–3·5 mm long, erect when young, deflexed when ripe, with short beaks and two stigmas. No bracts. Flowering period: May to June. Fruiting July.

Dioecious Sedge, the only dioecious species in the British Isles, occurs most often on rich, damp meadows, fens and base-rich flushes. The species is common in the British Isles, except in the south and east, and is to be found over most of the

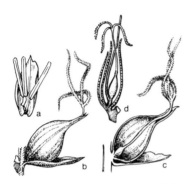

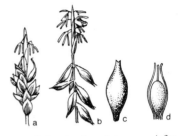

Flea Sedge (109) – (a) *young inflorescence*, (b) *mature inflorescence*, (c) *and* (d) *the utricle entire and in longitudinal section.* (a *and* b *2 ×*, c *and* d *4 × natural size.*)

Male and female flowers of two of the Carex *species*, (a)–(c) *Bottle sedge* (126), (d) *Bristle-Sedge. Male floret* (a) *in the glume*, (b) *female flower (really a one-flowered female inflorescence) surrounded by the utricle in the glume axis*, (c) *the same in section so that the style can be seen in full length and* (d) *the corresponding section through a female floret of the Bristle Sedge showing the bristle emerging from the utricle and attached to the base of the nut.* (a–c *4 ×*, d *5 × natural size.*)

Northern Hemisphere in both lowland and mountainous regions.

109   Flea Sedge
Carex pulicaris

Short-creeping, loosely tufted perennial with ascending rhizomes; stems 5–20 cm long, thin. Leaves narrow and bristle-shaped. The spike is male above and female below. No bracts.

The fruit is 4–6 mm long, shiny, dark brown, elliptic-ovate, plano-convex and almost winged, with a notched beak becoming pendulous at maturity. Flowering period: May to June. Fruiting June to July.

Flea Sedge grows in damp calcareous meadows, fens and base rich flushes. The species is common throughout the British Isles except in the south and east. It is also widespread throughout Europe.

Bristle Sedge
Carex microglochin

Short-creeping perennial, shoots often solitary; stems 5–15 cm long, stiff, erect, solid.

Leaves thick, still erect. The inflorescence is a few-flowered spike which bears male flowers uppermost and female flowers below. No bracts. Glumes about 2 mm long, oval. Utricles 4–6 mm, narrowly conical with a beak about 1 mm long; a stiff bristle arising from the base of the nut protrudes from the top of the beak. Flowering period: July. Fruiting August to September.

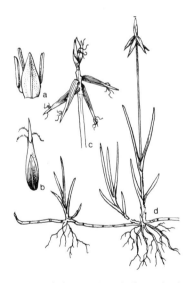

Bristle Sedge – (a) *male flower in the glume axis,* (b) *female utricle with the glume; note the emerging bristle,* (c) *the mature inflorescence and* (d) *the whole plant.* (a *and* b 4 ×, c 2 ×, d ½ × *natural size.*)

Bristle Sedge grows only on damp micaceous soil, in the Breadalbane district of Tayside, above 750 metres. It is more common in Scandinavia and the Arctic regions of the Northern Hemisphere.

110 Brown Sedge
Carex disticha

A perennial with deep-seated, horizontal, creeping rhizomes; stems single or in pairs 20–100 cm long, sharply triangular, rough. The leaves are thick, flat and rough beneath. The inflorescence is a dense chestnut-coloured panicle with spikes arranged in two rows on the axis. The spikes are numerous, the lowest and the uppermost female and the middle ones male. The utricles are 4–5 mm long, distinctly ribbed with narrow saw-edged wings and rough split beaks about 1 mm long. Flowering period: May to June. Fruiting July to August.

A plant of fens and marshes and meadows it is most frequent in eastern half of England and southern Scotland, apart from poor heath areas. The species is also widespread in the temperate zones of Europe and Asia. Can sometimes be mistaken for Sand Sedge (112)

143

Utricles of some Carex *species with similar inflorescences –* (a) *Brown Sedge (110),* (b) *Oval Sedge (111),* (c) *Sand Sedge (112),* (d) *Greater Tussock Sedge (113),* (e) *Fibrous Tussock Sedge (114),* (f) *Lesser Tussock Sedge (115) and* (g) *False Fox Sedge (116).* (*4 × natural size.*)

which also has scattered shoots. However, this species has a terminal spike and a hyaline inner face on the leaf sheath.

111　Oval Sedge
Carex ovalis

Densely tufted perennial; stems 10–90 cm long. Leaves narrow, flat. The inflorescence is a densely crowded head of three to nine comparatively large, greenish-brown, oval spikes. The lower bracts are bristle-like with the male flowers below and the female flowers above. The utricles are 4–5 mm long, pale brown, compressed, longitudinally nerved and provided with a membranous winged margin at the apex, and a rough bifid beak about 1 mm long. Flowering period: June. Fruiting July to August.

　Oval Sedge grows on moder-ately acid soil with poor drainage especially in meadows, on tracks, heaths and clearings in woods. It is qute common in the British Isles and the temperate regions of the Northern Hemisphere.

112　Sand Sedge
Carex arenaria

Scattered perennial with extensively-creeping rhizomes from which shoots emerge in rows at about every fourth node; the erect shoots consist of a tuft of narrow, stiff radical leaves and a stem 15–40 cm long. The inflorescence is oblong and spike-shaped up to 8 cm long and comprises six to twelve brownish spikes. The bracts are glume-like. The lower spikes are entirely female, the upper ones male and the middle ones both sexes, with the female flowers above. In maturity, the inflorescence becomes nodding. The utricle is flat, yellowish-brown, 4·5–5 mm long with a broad, membranous winged margin, serrate in the upper half, with a bifid beak up to 1·5 cm long. Flowering period: June to July. Fruiting July to August.

Sand Sedge grows in fixed dunes and on dry, sandy soil. Sand Sedge is a very effective sand binder, since the rhizomes can grow several metres a year. It is common around the coasts of the British Isles and inland on the Brecks and Lincoln heaths.

113 Greater Tussock or Paniculed Sedge
Carex paniculata

Very short rhizomatous perennial growing in large dense tussocks 1 metre in diameter, with stems 150 cm long and sharply triangular surrounded at the base by brownish-black leaf-sheaths. The leaves are long, spreading 3–7 mm wide and blue-green in colour. The inflorescence is a compact panicle 5–15 cm long, consisting of numerous greyish-brown spikes. Each spike bears many closely packed spikelets which are male above and female below, and at the bottom of the panicle some are wholly female. The female glumes are orange-brown, the utricles are 3–4 mm long, green to dark brown, only slightly ribbed; the beak is 1–1·5 mm long and serrate with a deep adaxial split. Flowering period: May to June. Fruiting July.

It grows in wet shady places on peaty base-rich soils in fens and beside slow moving streams. It is common throughout the British Isles and the temperate zones of the Northern Hemisphere.

114 Fibrous Tussock Sedge
Carex appropinquata

Is similar to 113 and 115, but is much more delicate and has narrower leaves, 1–2 mm wide, whose lower sheaths split longitudinally and form brownish-black, horsehair-like fibres. The inflorescence is 4–6 cm long and more compact, and the utricle is ovoid to subglobose with an unwinged beak. Flowering period: May to June. Fruiting June to July.

Fibrous Tussock Sedge grows in similar places to 113. The species is frequent in East Anglia and local in Yorkshire and West Neath. It is found in most northern and central European countries both in lowland and mountainous regions.

115 Lesser Tussock Sedge
Carex diandra

A short-creeping loosely tufted perennial; the stems are 25–40 cm long and delicate, cylindrical at the base, but triangular above. The leaf-sheaths are fibrous, shiny and brown. The inflorescence is 1–4 cm long and composed of several dark brown spikes which are male above and female below. The female glumes are about 3 mm long, broadly ovate, acute or mucronate. The utricle is 3–4 mm long, broadly ovate, or suborbicular, shiny, dark brown, only ribbed at the base and has a broad beak with finely toothed margins. Flowering period: May to June. Fruiting June to July.

Lesser Tussock Sedge grows in marshes and damp meadows and beside pools. The species is found scattered throughout the British Isles and the temperate areas of the Northern Hemisphere.

116 False Fox-Sedge
Carex otrubae

A stout densely tufted perennial; the stems are 30–100 cm long sharply triangular with flat faces. The leaves are 4–10 mm wide, bright green or becoming greyish-green when dry. The inflorescence is comprised of numerous yellowish-green or pale brown composite spikes. These consist of numerous spikelets up to 1 cm long, which are each male above and female below. The female glumes are 4–5 mm long, ovate, acuminate with a dark brown margin and a green mid-rib. The utricles are 5–6 mm long, at first green becoming yellowish-brown later, and are distinctly ribbed longitudinally especially on the back and have slightly rough, bifid beaks with serrelate margins. They are persistent at maturity, giving the panicle a very spiky appearance. Flowering period: June to July. Fruiting July to September.

False Fox-Sedge grows on clayey soils in damp grassy places, more rarely in drier places by roads and hedgebanks. The plant is common and generally distributed throughout the British Isles. It is common in Europe and Asia.

117 Remote Sedge
Carex remota

Short rhizomatous perennial;

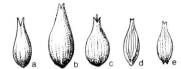

Utricles of some Carex *species with similar spikelets* – (a) *Remote Sedge (117)*, (b) *Spiked Sedge (118)*, (c) *Star Sedge (119)*, (d) *Elongated Sedge (120) and* (e) *White Sedge (121)*. *(4 × natural size.)*

shoots in dense tufts forming stools up to 30 cm high; stems 30–60 cm long, thin, somewhat limp, nodding at the top and bearing long, narrow leaves. The inflorescence is a quarter to a third of the length of the stem and composed of small, distantly spaced green spikes with leaf-like bracts. The individual spikes are female above, male below, though the lowest is often only female. The utricle is 2·5–3·5 mm long, plano-convex, elliptical, shiny green with a deeply cleaved beak about 0·5 mm long. Flowering period: June to July. Fruiting July to August.

Remote Sedge grows on damp clay or peat in woods, especially at the edges of slowly running springs, and in Alder or wet Birch carr. Common in lowland areas of the British Isles, and is also widespread in the temperate zones of the Northern Hemisphere.

118 Spiked Sedge
Carex spicata

A densely tufted perennial with short rhizomes; stems 30–70 cm long, triangular. The leaves are long and narrow, 2–4 mm wide. The lower sheaths form a false stem, pale brown below and are persistent. The inflorescence is spike-like, 1–4 cm long consisting of closely grouped spikes. These are greenish at first, later becoming dark brown and have male spikelets above and female ones below, although the lowest one can be entirely female. The utricles are 3–4 mm long, ovoid or broadly ellipsoid, green becoming shiny, dark brown at maturity; the beak is about 0·75 cm long and rough. Flowering period: June. Fruiting July to August.

Spiked Sedge grows beside ponds in scrub and dry grassy places. It occurs in central and northern areas of the British Isles and in temperate zones of the Northern Hemisphere.

119 Star Sedge
Carex echinata

A tufted perennial with very

short rhizomes; stems 10–40 cm long, stiff, triangular and striate. The leaves are narrow, shiny, dark green. The inflorescence is a composite series of spikes, 1–3 cm long, each consisting of three to five greenish, very closely placed spikelets, which are female at the apex and male below. The utricles are 3–4 mm long, pointed, star-shaped, which are green at first, and later golden brown, giving the spikelets a prickly appearance at maturity; the shortly cleft beaks are finely serrated. Flowering period: May to June. Fruiting June to August.

Star Sedge grows in damp acid marshes and meadows. The species is common in the north and west of the British Isles and widespread in cool and temperate zones of the Northern and Southern Hemispheres.

120   Elongated Sedge
Carex elongata

A densely tufted perennial with short rhizomes; stems 30–80 cm long. Leaves narrow, rough beneath, thin, more or less flat. The inflorescence is 3–7 cm long with somewhat separated erect, many-flowered, brownish spikes. The spikes are female at the top and male at the base, but the lowest spike is completely female. The lowest bracts are setaceous and the upper glumaceous. The female glumes of the spikelet are red-brown with green mid-ribs and whitish margins. The utricles are 3–4 mm long, lanceolate, distinctly ribbed, and are green at first, later becoming pale brown; the beak is truncate and finely serrated. Flowering period: May to June.

Elongated Sedge grows especially on damp soil in marshes, and open boggy woodland. The species is rather local in England and rare in Ireland, but more widespread in northern and central Europe and towards Siberia.

121   White Sedge
Carex curta

A loosely tufted perennial with short-creeping rhizomes; stems 25–50 cm long, sharply triangular and rough above. The leaves are soft, thin, flat, pale greyish-green. The inflorescence is 3–5 cm long, consisting of four to eight oblong, oval, whitish-grey contiguous or distant spikes. The spikelets are female above and male below. The female glumes are ovate or broadly elliptical, hyaline or whitish-green with green midribs. The utricles are 2–3 mm long, ' ovoid-ellipsoid, planoconvex, pale greenish or bluegreen to yellow with yellowish ribs; the beak is short, minutely rough, notched. Flowering period: July to August. Fruiting July to September.

White Sedge grows in damp meadows, bogs and acid fens. It is locally common throughout the British Isles but commoner in the north. The species is also widespread in the temperate zones of both the Northern and Southern Hemispheres.

122 Tufted Sedge
Carex elata

A large densely tufted bluegreen perennial; the stems are 45–100 cm long, rough, solid, stiff and sharply triangular. The leaves are 95–100 cm long by 4–6 mm wide, rough and stiff; the stems are invested at the base with a pointed, greyishbrown leaf-sheath, which eventually splits and becomes fibrous. The inflorescence consists of one or two male spikelets at the tip of the stem and two or three almost stemless, upright, female spikelets below; the uppermost female spikelet often has some male flowers at the top. The female glumes are 3–4 mm long, ovate, elliptic with hyaline margins. The utricles are 3–4 mm long, elliptical, ribbed, greenish; the beak is 0·2 mm long, truncate. Flowering period: May to June. Fruiting June.

Tufted Sedge is a species of fens with seasonal flooding and is common by ditches, rivers and lakes. It plays an important role in the overgrowth of lakes and can form large stands on the muddy soil of marshes.

With age, the tufts become very broad and tall. They die in the centre, but continue to grow at the edges. In the dead tufts Alder and Willow can grow and the *Carex* marsh gradually becomes carr. The species is fairly common in the fertile areas of the British Isles and is also widespread in Europe, apart from the extreme northern and southern zones.

123 Common Sedge
Carex nigra

A solitary or tufted perennial with far-creeping rhizomes; the stems can be either stiff and erect, or somewhat bow-shaped and upward reaching at the base; they are 7–70 cm long,

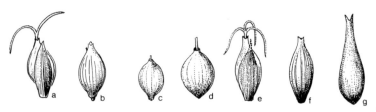

Female florets and utricles of various Carex *species – (a) and (b)* Tufted Sedge *(122), (c)* Common Sedge *(123), (d)* Slender Tufted Sedge *(124), (e) and (f)* Lesser Pond Sedge *(see page 151) and (g)* Greater Pond Sedge *(125). (4 × natural size.)*

triangular, slender and solid. The leaves are up to 20 cm long, 2–3 mm wide, blue-green. The inflorescence consists of one or two male spikes at the apex and two or three greenish-black, sessile or very short-stemmed upright, oblong cylindrical female spikes. The female glumes are 2·5–3·5 mm long, lanceolate-oblong with a narrow hyaline margin. The utricle is 2·5–3·5 mm long, flat, elliptical, greenish with feint ribs and practically no beak. Flowering period: May to June. Fruiting June to August.

Common Sedge is the most frequent of our native sedges. It is found everywhere on damp soil, but usually in enriched marshes and bogs, and low-lying meadows. It is very widely distributed in the British Isles and the temperate zones of the Northern Hemisphere, both in lowland and mountainous areas. It has also been reported from the southern tip of South America and as an adventive in Australia.

124 Slender Tufted Sedge
Carex acuta

A tufted perennial with long, far-creeping rhizomes; the stems are 60–120 cm long, stiff, erect and sharply triangular. The leaves are up to 140 cm long and up to 7 mm wide, somewhat limp, distinctly folded and dark green. The inflorescence can be between one sixth and one quarter of the length of the stem, consisting of one to three long, narrow male spikes above and two to four female spikes below, of which the uppermost can have a few male flowers at the top; these are elongated, cylindrical (3–10 cm long), first upright, later nodding and black or green mottled in colour. The female spikes have long, leaf-like bracts and the lowest overtops the inflorescence. The female glumes are 2·5-4 mm long and oblong-ovate. The utricle is 2-3·5 mm long, flat, broadly elliptical and green with feint ribs and hardly any beak. Flowering period: May to June. Fruiting June to July.

Slender Tufted Sedge is a characteristic member of ponds, dykes and riversides or woodland marshes with a high water table. It is found scattered throughout the British Isles, but mainly in the south and west. It is also widespread in the temperate zones of the Northern Hemisphere.

Slender Tufted Sedge may easily be mistaken for the similar, Lesser Pond Sedge, *Carex acutiformis*, which grows in similar places and can be identified by having three stigmas, convex utricles, 3-5 mm long, with distinct ribs and a very short bifid beak.

125 Greater Pond Sedge
Carex riparia

A similar growth habit to Slender Tufted Sedge (124), but more robust with stems 80-150 cm long and stiff, upright, somewhat blue-green leaves, 6-15 mm wide. The inflorescence is very long; it can be up to nearly one third of the length of the stem and consists of three to six closely placed male spikes and three to five thick, dark green distant female spikes. The upper one is sessile and upright, whilst the lower ones have stems and become nodding. The somewhat inflated oval, brownish utricle is 6-8 mm long and with a distinct bifid beak. Flowering period: May to June. Fruiting June to September.

Greater Pond Sedge grows in similar places to 123 and 124 and has about the same distribution in the British Isles. The species is also widespread throughout most of Europe, apart from the extreme north and is found in northern Africa and western Asia.

126 Bottle Sedge
Carex rostrata

A sparsely tufted perennial with far-creeping rhizomes; the stems are 20-100 cm long, blue-green, triangular, smooth below and rough above. The leaves are 30-120 cm long and 2-7 mm wide with inrolled margins. The inflorescence is up to half the length of the stem; the bracts are long, leaf-like and usually reach up to the top of the inflorescence; there are one to four male spikes and two to five yellowish-green, cylindrical upright female spikes. The inflated oval utricles abruptly terminate in an elongated bifid beak. Flowering period: June to July. Fruiting July to September.

Bottle Sedge grows in wet peaty places and can form extensive stands at the edges of lakes, ponds, peat bogs and ditches. It is easily recognised from a distance by the bluish-green leaves. Common throughout the British Isles and widespread in the Northern Hemisphere.

127 Bladder Sedge
Carex vesicaria

Similar to 126, but differs by the sharply triangular stems, with comparatively broad, pale green leaves, and the long, oval fairly thick female spikes, and oblique, open yellowish-green or brownish-green utricles. These are inflated, bladder-shaped, 6–8 mm long, gradually narrowing into a long, pointed, deeply bifid beak. Flowering period: June. Fruiting July to August.

Bladder Sedge grows in dense stands in boggy places, especially on fertile soil, in wet woods, edges of streams and around lakes. It is scattered throughout the British Isles and

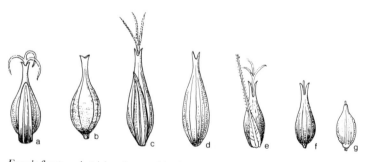

Female florets and utricles of some of the different Carex *species –* (a) *and* (b) *Bottle Sedge* (126), (c) *and* (d) *Bladder Sedge* (127), (e) *and* (f) *Cyperus Sedge* (128) *and* (g) *Pendulous Sedge* (129). (4 × *natural size.*)

is also widespread in the temperate zones of the Northern Hemisphere.

128 Cyperus Sedge
Carex pseudocyperus

A loosely tufted perennial with short rhizomes; the stems are 40–90 cm long, rough and sharply triangular. The leaves are broad, pale yellowish-green and longer than the stems. The inflorescence is one sixth to one quarter the length of the stem; the bracts are leaf-like and the lowest three to four times longer than the stem and consists of a single male spike and closely clustered three to five cylindrical female spikes below. These are up to 6 cm long, all of which hang to one side on long, thin stalks. The female glumes are 5–10 mm long, ovate brownish hyaline, with a green mid-rib drawn out to a long thin bristle. The utricles are 4–5 mm long, broader than the glumes, shiny yellowish-green, ovoid-ellipsoid, ribbed and falling easily at maturity; the beak is long, pointed and deeply bifid. Flowering period: May to June. Fruiting July to August.

This species is easily distinguished from other native *Carex* species by the yellowish-green colour and the elegant pendant female spikes.

Cyperus Sedge grows in marshes and at the edges of ponds and slow-moving streams. It can be found occasionally in stagnant water in woods, as it can tolerate some shade. It is local in the British Isles, occurring mainly in the south and is widespread in the temperate zones of the Northern Hemisphere and even New Zealand.

129 Pendulous Sedge
Carex pendula

A short rhizomatous perennial growing in large dense tufts up to 70 cm in diameter; the stems are 60–180 cm long, trigonous. The leaves are 20–100 cm long and 15–20 mm wide with reddish-brown sheaths below. The inflorescence is about half the length of the stem with leaf-like bracts nearly reaching the apex, and consisting of a single male spike above and four or five female spikes below; the female spikes are 7–16 cm long, cylindrical, erect at first, but later become bow-shaped and pendulous. The female glumes are 2–2·5 mm long, ovate, red-brown with a pale mid-rib. The utricles are 3–3·5 mm long, greyish-green, later becoming brown, ribless, elliptical; the beaks are short and truncate. Flowering period: May to June. Fruiting June to July.

Pendulous Sedge cannot be mistaken for any other species on account of its size. It grows in damp woods and on shady stream banks with damp clayey soil and is locally abundant in the south, but rare in the north of the British Isles. The species is also widespread from Denmark southwards through Europe and to northern Africa and into the warm, temperate zones of parts of Asia.

130 Slender Sedge
Carex lasiocarpa

A slender, loosely tufted perennial with far-creeping rhizomes; the stems are 45–120 cm long, slender, stiff, trigonous, smooth or slightly rough above and invested at the base with reddish-brown sheaths. The leaves are thread-like, 30–100 cm by 1–2 mm, greyish-green and inrolled. The inflorescence is one eighth to one sixth the length of the stem with leaf-like bracts often exceeding the apex and consisting of one or two long, thin male spikes and two to four distant, oblong female

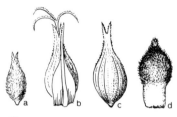

The variety of hairy utricles found in some Carex *species – (a) Slender Sedge (130), (b) and (c) female floret and utricle of Hairy Sedge (131) and (d) utricle of Pill Sedge (132) showing the oily texture at the base of the ovary. (a–c 4 ×, d 5 × natural size.)*

spikes. The female glumes are 3·5–4·5 mm long, lanceolate, chestnut-brown with a pale mid-rib. The utricle is 3·5–4·5 mm long, oval, tomentose and grey-green; the beak is short and deeply bifid. Flowering period: June to July. Fruiting July to September.

Slender Sedge grows on the sandy banks of lakes, in mires and marshes. At times it can form pure, extensive stands. It is easily recognised, even in the vegetative state, on account of the thread-like greyish-green leaves, with red sheaths at the base. It is found scattered throughout the British Isles and is widespread in the temperate zones of the Northern Hemisphere.

131 Hairy Sedge
Carex hirta

A tufted perennial with horizontal far-creeping rhizomes; the stems are 15–70 cm long, trignous, with rounded faces. The leaves are 10–50 cm long, 2–5 mm wide, greyish-mid-green, hairy. The inflorescence is up to three quarters the length of the stem; the lower bracts are leaf-like, longer than the spike but not exceeding the inflorescence and consisting of two or three tightly clustered male spikes above and two or three oblong, fairly fat, upright distant female spikes below. The female glumes are 6–8 mm long, ovate-oblong, green hyaline, with a mid-rib decurrent with an awn. The utricle is 5–7 mm long, oval, finely hairy; the beak has a bifid apex. Flowering period: May to June. Fruiting June to September.

Hairy Sedge is one of the few native sedges with hairy leaves, and should therefore be easily recognised, although there are some varieties which have almost completely smooth leaves. One can recognise them by the relatively large hairy utricles. It can be found in many different places, on both damp and dry soils. It can grow in sand dunes, meadows, hedge banks, along dry roadsides and well-trodden paths and on the fringes of commons and woods. It is common throughout the British Isles and is also widespread in Europe, northern Africa and northern Asia.

132 Pill Sedge
Carex pilulifera

A densely tufted perennial with short rhizomes; the stems are comparatively short, 10–30 cm, wiry, trigonous, more or less rough above. The leaves are 5–20 cm long by 1·3–2 mm wide, rough above and more or less flat. The inflorescence is 2–4 cm long and tightly clustered at the tip of the stem; it consists of a thin, solitary male spike and two to four nearly spherical greenish female spikes. The female glumes are 3–3·5 mm long, broadly ovate, red-brown, hyaline towards the margin, with a green mid-rib. The utricle is 2–3·5 mm long, finely hairy, roundish; the beak is short and notched. Flowering period: May to June. Fruiting June to July.

Pill Sedge is a plant of dry leached, skeletal or peaty soils. It grows in woods and on the slopes of heaths and commons.

The species occurs throughout the British Isles but is more common on sandy soils and is widespread in Europe and northern Asia.

133 Glaucous Sedge
Carex flacca

A loosely tufted perennial with often far-creeping horizontal rhizomes; the stems are 10–60 cm long, smooth, bluntly triangular. The leaves are up to 50 cm long and 2–4 mm wide, stiff, flat, which are green above and bluish-green below, most noticeable on the inrolled leaves. The inflorescence is one fifth to one third of the length of the stem; the bracts are leaf-like and slightly exceed the inflorescence; it consists of one to three male spikes and two to five close-flowered reddish-black, cylindrical female spikes, of which the uppermost is upright and relatively short-stemmed, whilst the others have longer stems and become nodding. The female glumes are 2–3 mm long, oblong-ovate, purple-black, pruinose with a wide pale midrib and hyaline margin with a mucronate apex. The utricles are elliptical, first yellowish-green, later reddish-black, 2–3 mm long. They have a fine papillose surface; the beak is very short and truncate. Flowering period: May to June. Fruiting June to September.

Glaucous Sedge grows on dry calcareous grassland, in damp clayey woods, marshes and fens. It is common throughout the British Isles, except on very poor soils. It is also widespread in Europe, northern Africa, western and northern Asia and has been found adventitiously in North America.

The inflorescences of two commonly confused Carex *species* – (a) *Glaucous Sedge (133) and* (b) *Carnation Sedge (134). (⅔ × natural size.)*

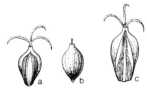

Female florets and utricles of some Carex *species* – (a) *and* (b) *Glaucous Sedge (133),* (c) *and* (d) *Carnation Sedge (134),* (e), (f) *and* (g) *Long-Stalked Yellow Sedge (135).* (4 × *natural size.*)

Glaucous Sedge together with the Common Sedge (123) and Carnation Sedge (134) belong to the most common 'small sedges' found in the British Isles. Common Sedge can be distinguished from Glaucous Sedge, by having upright, practically sessile spikes and smaller utricles.

134 Carnation Sedge
Carex panicea

A tufted perennial with short, horizontal, creeping rhizomes; the stems are 10–60 cm long, often curved above, trigonous-subterete striate. The leaves are up to 60 cm by 1–5 mm wide, blue-green or pale grey-green at the base. The inflorescence is one sixth to a quarter the length of the stem and consists of loose leaf-like bracts one or two times as long as the spike – a single male spike above and one to three upright or slightly open few-flowered female spikes below. The female glumes are 3–4 mm long, broadly ovate, purple or red-brown with pale mid-ribs and hyaline margins. The utricles are 3–4 mm long, broadly obovoid and inflated on the adaxial side, olive-green, later brownish; the beak is short and truncate. Flowering period: May to June. Fruiting June to September.

Carnation Sedge grows in damp meadows, fens and marshes. It is common in the British Isles and the Northern Hemisphere, both in fertile and poor soils.

135 Long-Stalked Yellow Sedge
Carex lepidocarpa

A loosely tufted perennial with up to four shoots and short

rhizomes; the stems are 20–75 cm long, trigonous, solid. The leaves are 10–40 cm long, 2–3 mm wide, keeled, mid- to yellowish-green or straw-coloured when dead. The inflorescence is one tenth to a quarter the length of the stem; the bracts leaf-like or glumaceous exceeding the inflorescence. It consists of a single, long-stemmed, angled male spike at the apex and two or three spherical to oval female spikes of which the upper two are often sessile and crowded, the third with a short stalk and found halfway down the stem. The female glumes are shed before the utricle; they are 2·5–4 mm long, ovate-lanceolate, orange or red-brown with a green mid-rib and often hyaline margin. The utricles are 3–5 mm long, yellowish green, faintly ribbed, well-inflated below, with a long pointed bifid beak. Flowering period: May to June. Fruiting July to August.

Long-Stalked Yellow Sedge grows in damp meadows, fens and marshes with base-rich soils. It is common in suitable habitats in the British Isles and is widespread in the temperate zones of the Northern Hemisphere.

The yellowish-green tuft-forming *Carex* species with nearly spherical, prickly female spikes have caused many problems of classification. There are many overlapping varieties and races, which readily produce hybrids. Sometimes they are put in the Yellow Sedges or *Carex flava* group.

136 Wood Sedge
Carex sylvatica

A densely tufted perennial with very short rhizomes; the stems are 20–60 cm long, slender, triangular above, spreading or nodding. The leaves are 5–60 cm by 3–4 mm soft, keeled or plicate, bright green. The inflorescence is one third to half the length of the stem with lowermost bracts longer than the inflorescence and consisting of a single male spike and three to six narrow, thin, distant female spikes on long stalks. The female glumes are 3–5 mm long, ovate-lanceolate, hyaline, straw-coloured or brown with a green mid-rib and pointed apex. The utricles are 4–5 mm long, ellipsoid or obovoid-trigonous, green with two prominent lateral nerves; the beak is 1–1·5 mm long, bifid. Flowering period: May to July.

Pale Sedge (Carex pallescens) – (a) *panicle*, (b) *female floret and* (c) *utricle. Wood Sedge (136)* – (d) *female floret and* (c) *utricle. Spring Sedge (137)* – (f) *utricle.* (a ⅓ × b f 4 × *natural size.*)

Fruiting May to August.

Wood Sedge grows on heavy wet soils in shady woods, although sometimes on chalky soils. It is common in Beech woods throughout the British Isles, and also widespread in the temperate zones of the Northern Hemisphere.

137 Spring Sedge
Carex caryophyllea

A loosely tufted perennial with short horizontal rhizomes; the stems are 2–30 cm long, trigonous and leafy below. The leaves are up to 20 cm by 1·5–2·5 mm wide, somewhat reflexed, rough on the upper surface, shiny, more or less flat mid- or dark green. The inflorescence is 2–4 cm long, the lower bracts often leaf-like, the upper glumaceous, consisting of a solitary male spike and 2–3 oblong, female spikes. The female glumes are 2–2·5 mm long, broadly ovate, red-brown with an excurrent green mid-rib. The utricles are 2–3 mm long and downy, obovoid, olive-green; the beak is short and notched. Flowering period: April to May. Fruiting May to July.

Spring Sedge grows on dry banks, ditches and at roadsides. It may also be found on open ground on heaths, but does not thrive where the soil is too poor. It is found throughout the British Isles and is also widespread in Europe and northern Asia, both in lowland and mountainous districts.

THE RUSH FAMILY – JUNCACEAE

RUSHES

The species belonging to the genus *Juncus* are distinguishable

159

from grasses and sedges by their perfect flowers. These are individually arranged in many- or few-flowered inflorescences rather than into modified spikelets.

Rushes have six dry membranous segments in the perianth arranged into two whorls of three, usually six stamens, also in two whorls, and a single pistil, which consists of a trilocular ovary and a style, which divides into three long, thread-like stigmas. The fruit is a capsule containing many, small lightweight seeds, whose testas become glutinous when wet. The sticky testa is thought to be an aid to seed-dispersal as it can easily get caught in the fur of passing animals or on the feet and feathers of birds.

The trimerous whorls of the rush flower are very similar to the more showy members of the Monocotyledons such as a Tulip flower. However, unlike the insect-pollinated petaloid monocots, rushes, like grasses and sedges, rely on wind-pollination for fertilisation, hence their rather inconspicuous small 'glume-like' perianths.

The perianths are persistent and continue to invest the capsule at maturity.

As is the case with most other wind-pollinated plants with bisexual flowers, rushes are protogynous, which means that the stigmas develop and are ready to receive pollen from other flowers before their own anthers begin to shed pollen. In this way self-pollination is avoided. Most insect-pollinated flowers are, by contrast protandrous, whereby the anthers develop and shed pollen before the stigmas become receptive.

Rushes are extremely variable in vegetative morphology, but they possess several unique features. Their stems are usually cylindrical in cross-section, have no nodes, and are filled with a spongy pith, which may sometimes be interrupted with air chambers, so that it appears to have narrow walls across a hollow stem. The leaves are smooth, almost cylindrical and usually gulley-shaped. They invest the stem with a partially enclosed sheath, whose margins are still visible. The inside of the blade, in a similar way to the stem, can be filled with pith or filled with air chambers interrupted by transverse walls.

Juncus comprises about 300 species, about twenty-six of which occur in the British Isles.

138 Soft Rush
Juncus effusus

Perennial; stems densely tufted, robust, glossy green, 30–150 cm long and invested with dark reddish-brown sheaths at the base. It is cylindrical with 40–90 striae, and filled with a continuous spongy pith. The open, richly branched inflorescence is apparently laterally orientated on the stem, due to the long bract which subtends it. The inflorescence is lax with branches of different lengths or nearly spherical and invariably pale brown in colour. Flowers with three stamens. Flowering period: June to September.

Soft Rush is very common throughout the British Isles in damp soil, e.g. wet pastures, bogs, and damp woods. The plant can be a troublesome weed on waterlogged pastures. Animals do not like to eat the stiff stems and its presence suppresses the development of the fodder grasses. It often grows in clearings in woods, when the soil is less rich after tree-felling. In historical times, the pith was scraped out of the stem and used for making candle wicks, or the tough stems were used for basket work. The species is widespread in the temperate

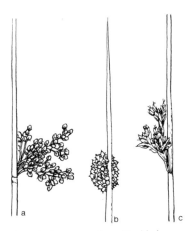

Three indigenous rushes with side-borne inflorescences – (a) Soft Rush (138), (b) Conglomerate Rush (139) and (c) Thread Rush (140). ($\frac{2}{3}$ × natural size.)

zones of both the Northern and Southern Hemispheres.

139 Conglomerate Rush
Juncus conglomeratus

Similar to 138 in habit, but not with such thick tufts. Stems 30–80 cm long, finely striate, somewhat rough, matt green and invested with pale brown sheaths below. The compact inflorescence is very densely-flowered with short branches, almost spherical. Flowering period: May to July.

Conglomerate Rush grows in similar habitats to 138 and is

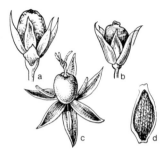

Capsules surrounded by the persistent perianth of (a) *Soft Rush (138) and* (b) *Conglomerate Rush (139) with* (c) *the flower and* (d) *the seed of the latter. The seed is illustrated as when damp with the outer layer of the seed-wall transformed into a glutinous mucous membrane.* (a–c 4 × , d 23 × *natural size.*)

just as common in the British Isles. It is also widespread in most of Europe, northern Africa and Asia. Like Soft Rush its stems have been used for the similar practical purpose of basket work.

Conglomerate Rush is readily distinguished from 138 by its capsule being shorter than the perianth segments, and with a rather obtuse apex.

140 Thread Rush
Juncus filiformis

A delicate, perennial plant with creeping rhizomes from which develop rows of fine stems about

1 mm in diameter. Stems 15–45 cm long, leafless, bearing a few-flowered inflorescence of pale brown flowers at the mid-point. The inflorescence bract is as long as the stem. The perianth segments are whitish-green. The capsule is nearly spherical with a sharp apex and is as long as the perianth. Flowering period: July to August.

Thread Rush grows on poor, damp soil. It is very local and is found in the Lake District and a few places in Scotland on stony lake shores. It is widespread in temperate zones throughout the world.

141 Blunt-Flowered Rush
Juncus subnodulosus

Perennial with far-creeping horizontal rhizomes; stems 50–120 cm long, rather soft and bright green, in patches, leaves similar. The stems are hollow, but with transverse and longitudinal walls. Sterile stems with one leaf, flowering stems with one or two leaves, each with thirty-five to sixty transverse walls. The inflorescence is terminal and repeatedly compound, of many heads of three to twelve closely grouped pale brown flowers. Secondary branches widely diverging.

Perianth segments are blunt and have a broad, silvery white, membranous margin. The broad, oval beaked capsule may be slightly longer than the perianth. Flowering period: July to September.

Blunt-Flowered Rush grows in fens, marshes, dune-slacks, and on calcareous peat. Locally abundant northwards to southern Scotland and the Hebrides. Blunt-Flowered Rush seldom produces viable seed, but it is able to reproduce large stands of vegetative annual shoots. The species is widespread over most of Europe, northern Africa and the Near East.

142 Jointed Rush
Juncus articulatus

Perennial with upright, or short, creeping rhizomes from which extend tufts of arc-shaped shoots; stems erect 15–60 cm long. Stiff bearing two to seven laterally flattened, curved, hollow leaves, with eighteen to twenty-five transverse walls. The inflorescence is repeatedly compound, terminal, the branches diverging at an acute angle and culminating in a head of four to eight dark chestnut, or almost black,

flowers. The narrow, membranous margined perianth segments are considerably shorter than the sharply pointed, shiny, brownish-black capsule. The three perianth segments of the outer whorl are broader and less sharply pointed than those of the inner whorl. Flowering period: July to September.

Jointed Rush grows everywhere on wet ground, e.g. in wet pastures, in marshes, waterlogged fields, at the edges of ponds, in ditches and dunes, but preferably on rich soil. It is common in the British Isles and temperate areas of the Northern and Southern Hemispheres.

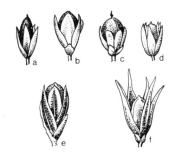

Capsules surrounded by the persistent perianth of various Rush species – (a) Jointed Rush (142), (b) Mud Rush (143), (c) Round-Fruited Rush (see page 164), (d) Bulbous Rush (see page 164), (e) Health Rush (see page 165) and (f) Toad Rush (see page 165). (3 × natural size.)

Bulbous Rush
Juncus bulbosus

Small, grass-like densely tufted perennial; stems thread-like 5–20 cm long, slightly bulbous at the base. The leaves thread-like and bristle-shaped with many indistinct transverse walls. The stem culminates in an open tassle-shaped inflorescence consisting of small reddish-brown or greenish heads on diverging branches. The three perianth segments of the outer whorl are pointed and those of the inner whorl obtuse. The capsule is bluntly triangular and about the same length as the perianth. Flowering period: July to September.

Bulbous Rush is a polymorphic plant which grows both on damp soil and in nutrient deficient water near the edges of ponds. On very wet soil, the stems are prostrate and form roots at the nodes. When underwater, the basal leaves are long and slender, and the stems are much branched. It is widespread throughout the British Isles, and is a characteristic species of poor acid soils on heaths, bogs, woodland rides and cart tracks. It is also widespread in Europe and northern Africa.

143 Mud Rush
Juncus gerardii

Tufted perennial with creeping rhizomes; stems 10–40 cm long, erect, cylindrical bearing very narrow gulley-shaped leaves without dividing walls. Most of the leaves extend from the base of the stem; one or two are to be found emerging from the middle. The flowers are grouped in a glistening, brown, terminal, tassle-shaped inflorescence. The perianth segments have blunt tips and are the same length as the oval capsule. Flowering period: June to July.

Mud Rush grows as a compact, green sward. It is native of salt marshes and often dominant in the upper parts. It is found abundantly along the coasts of the British Isles and rarely inland. It is widespread in temperate areas of the Northern Hemisphere. It is an important fodder plant, which produces fine rich hay.

The closely related Round-Fruited Rush, *Juncus compressus*, is distinguished from 143 by its flattened stems and short perianth leaves, which are about half the length of the capsule. It is quite common on damp, rich inland soils of marshes and alluvial meadows.

Heath Rush
Juncus squarrosus

Tough wiry perennial, in dense low tufts. Stems 10–50 cm long,

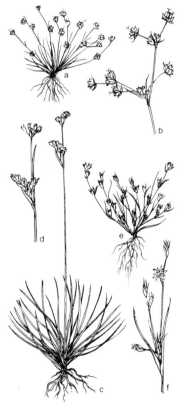

very stiff, completely leafless or bearing just a single basal leaf. The leaves are stiff, bristle-shaped and invest the base of the stems. The inflorescence is terminal, glistening, greyish-brown, and has erect uneven branches, of which the longest is just about the same length as the inflorescence bract. The peri-anth segments are brown with a white, membranous margin. The capsule is yellowish-brown, acutely pointed, oval and about the length of the perianth. Flowering period: June to July.

Heath Rush is a plant of poor, acid soil, growing on damp heaths moors and bogs. It is abundant on suitable soils in the British Isles. The species is a common inhabitant of the Atlantic coastal areas in Europe and northern Africa.

Toad Rush
Juncus bufonius

A slender annual; stems 3–25 cm long, thread-like, richly branched, pale green later brownish. The leaves are thin and narrow. The spikelets are up to 5 mm long, greenish-white and scattered along the branches either singly or in groups of two or three. The capsule is oblong and noticeably

Habits and inflorescences of (a) *and* (b) *Bulbous Rush (see page 164),* (c) *and* (d) *Heath Rush (see page 165),* (e) *and* (f) *Toad Rush (see page 165).* (a, c *and* e $\frac{1}{3}$ ×, b, d *and* f $\frac{2}{3}$ × *natural size.*)

shorter than the narrow pointed perianth segments. Flowering period: May to September.

Toad Rush grows at the edges of ponds, streams, ditches, in wheel ruts and in open damp soil. On low, waterlogged arable land it can be a trouble-some weed and during wet seasons can occur in quantity in spring corn and root crops. The species is common throughout the British Isles and is also widespread throughout much of the World.

WOODRUSH

Plants which belong to the Woodrush genus, *Luzula*, are perennial herbs and may be identified by their flat, grass-like leaves with long, soft hairs at the margins, which invest the stems with a closed sheath. Woodrushes can always be distinguished from grasses because their leaves are placed in three rows up the stem rather than in two rows. The flowers are similar to *Juncus* except that the fruit is a one-celled capsule containing only three seeds. The seeds are provided with a whitish appendage containing a rich oil, thought to be much sought after by ants. Most species of Woodrush, like *Juncus*, have seeds which become glutinous when wet.

There are about eighty species of Woodrush, ten of which are found in the British Isles.

144 Greater Woodrush
Luzula sylvatica

Robust perennial growing in large tufts or mats with short stocks and numerous stolons. Radical leaves over 1 cm wide, stiff and pointed, shiny dark green, sparsely hairy. Stems 30–80 cm long culminating in a large and richly branched, composite inflorescence. Flowers chestnut-brown, in clusters of three or four heads. Perianth segments lanceolate about equalling the pointed oval capsule. Flowering period: May to June.

Greater Woodrush grows on peaty soil in woods (especially Oak woods) and open moorland. The plant is found scattered, where it often forms large stands. It can be found throughout the British Isles, but is more abundant in the west and north. It has a distinctly Atlantic distribution off the west coasts of Europe.

145 Hairy Woodrush
Luzula pilosa

Tufted perennial growing in dense tufts with short stock and slender stolons. Radical leaves 3–4 mm wide with long white hairs on the margins, and small swelling at the tips. The flowering stems are 15–30 cm long, culminating in an open, tassel-shaped inflorescence. Flowers are usually single on long peduncles, which after flowering diverge from each other.

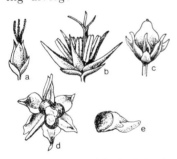

Broad-leaved Hairy Woodrush (145) – (a) and (b) flower, (a) female in receptive stage, (b) at anthesis, (c) a closed capsule surrounded by the persistent perianth, (d) an open capsule containing three seeds. (a, b, c and d 3 ×, e 4 × natural size.)

The perianth segments are dark chestnut-brown with a white membranous margin. They invest the ripe capsule at maturity, but are shorter than the capsule. Flowering period: April to June.

This is one of our earliest flowering woodland plants. The leaves are green throughout the year.

Hairy Woodrush grows most often on peaty soil in deciduous woods and hedge banks throughout the British Isles, Europe and Asia.

146 Field Woodrush
Luzula campestris

Loosely tufted perennial with horizontal creeping stolons. Leaves 2–4 mm wide with a small swelling at the tip. Stems 5–20 cm long culminating in a loose inflorescence of one sessile and three to six pedunculate spherical flowerheads each with up to twelve flowers. Flowers chestnut-brown. Perianth segments longer than the obovoid capsule.

Field Woodrush grows on open, grassy places. It is very common throughout the British Isles and widespread in temperate areas such as Europe and Asia.

167

147 Many-Flowered Woodrush

Luzula multiflora

Very similar to 146, but is more tufted, has taller stems, 20–40 cm long and has an inflorescence of ten ovate or elongate eight- to sixteen-flowered clusters on straight slender branches. Flowering period: May to June.

Many-Flowered Woodrush grows preferably on acid, peaty soils, e.g. on heaths and poor pastures in woods and amongst undergrowth. It is common throughout the British Isles and widespread in temperate zones of the Northern and Southern Hemispheres.

BIBLIOGRAPHY

Clapham, A. R., Tutin, T. G. and Warburg, E. F., *Flora of the British Isles* ed. 2, 1269 pp., Cambridge University Press, 1962.

Hegi, G., *Illustrierte Flora von Mittel-Europa* ed. 1, 1:165–402, 2:5–184, Lehmann, 1907–9.

Hubbard, C. E., *Grasses* ed. 2, 462 pp., Penguin, 1976.

Jermy, A. C. and Tutin, T. G., *British Sedges*, 199 pp., Botanical Society of the British Isles, 1968.

Keeble-Martin, W., *The Concise British Flora in Colour*, 231 pp., George Rainbird, 1967.

Moore, I., *Grasses and Grasslands*, 175 pp., Collins, 1966.

Ross-Craig, S., *Drawings of British Plants* 30:plates 1–32, Cambridge University Press, 1973.

Tutin, T. G. *et al.*, *Flora Europaea* vol. 5 in press, Cambridge University Press, 1978.

INDEX OF LATIN NAMES

The figures in **bold** refer to illustration numbers

INDEX OF ENGLISH NAMES

The figures in **bold** refer to illustration numbers